# Smile Please

*By the same Author*

NINETEEN TO THE DOZEN
GIRLS WILL BE GIRLS
I SAY!
I'LL LET YOU KNOW
(*Musings from Myrtlebank*)

*Edited by Arthur Marshall*

NEW STATESMAN COMPETITIONS
SALOME, DEAR, *NOT* IN THE FRIDGE
NEVER RUB BOTTOMS WITH A PORCUPINE

# ARTHUR MARSHALL

# *Smile Please*

*FURTHER MUSINGS FROM MYRTLEBANK*

*Illustrated by Tim Jaques*

HAMISH HAMILTON
London

First published in Great Britain 1982
by Hamish Hamilton Ltd
Garden House 57–59 Long Acre London WC2E 9JZ

Copyright © 1977, 1978, 1979, 1980, 1981 by Arthur Marshall
Illustrations copyright © 1982 by Tim Jaques

British Library Cataloguing in Publication Data

Marshall, Arthur, 1910–
   Smile please.
   I. Title
   828'.91407     PR6063.A67
   ISBN 0-241-10842-X

Typeset by Rowland Phototypesetting Ltd
Bury St Edmunds, Suffolk
Printed in Great Britain by
St Edmundsbury Press, Bury St Edmunds, Suffolk

to
Teresa Rothschild
and
Patricia Llewelyn-Davies
with love

# Acknowledgements

Once more, I am grateful to the Editor of the *New Statesman* for his permission to reprint these pieces, all of which appeared originally in that magazine.

ARTHUR MARSHALL

# Contents

# Tit and tat

My high standards of propriety and decorum are already so well known to readers that I hardly need to repeat how distasteful it is for me to be concerned with anything verging, however remotely, on 'smut'. The dire statements dished out to me from about the age of 9 to 18 (nobody ever mentioned 'smut' at Cambridge so I assumed that by then we were all safe) have led to the fastidiousness that has been, I do so hope, a pleasing feature of this column, a living proof that I have paid attention to the bituminous warning in Ecclesiasticus about getting defiled (XIII, 1 if you care to refresh your memories). But every so often a time comes when, alas, facts must be faced and a kind correspondent from the London area has drawn my attention to an unusual matter concerning motor-cars and their registrations, namely that he has never in his life seen anywhere a number-plate bearing the letters BUM.

Is there, he wonders, somewhere deep in the, pardon me, bowels of the Ministry of Transport an official adjudicator, certainly not in Holy Orders and obviously specially selected for impurity of mind, to whom all potential combinations of car letterings are submitted and who, with a little Tch! Tch! of dismay and a pursing of the lips, disallows such infelicities as ARS. Is he, I ask myself, in close touch with representative members of the Stock Exchange, those legendary figures who were alleged to divide their time between cornering Consols, or whatever, and inventing smutty jokes, figures who might be relied upon to help him pronounce a sensible and final verdict on, perhaps, BAG and BRA.

How jolly to picture an ordinary working day in the life of our adjudicator, a Mr Willmott, as he enters his office, his eyes recently caressed by the sight, in the street outside, of motor-car number-plates bearing a few of his own personal and image-creating favourites — COT, DEN, GEM, SKY, HAY and JIG.

Confident that all is well in his department (yesterday they considered and rejected CAD and OAF), he seats himself and presses the buzzer and to him there enters his secretary, Miss Lightbody, clutching her Jotto scribbling-pad and looking flustered. 'Oh Mr Willmott, I do hope I've done the right thing but after you'd left yesterday they rang up from the Wolverhampton depot to say that they were right out of registrations – you remember we gave them ELF and ODE only a year ago but there's been such a run on Hondas and Volvos that they've used them all up – and they asked if this time they could have something more solid and, well, earthy and could they use SOD? So I hurried to my Chambers and found that sod is a turf, usually cut in rectangular shape, and so I said yes. Is it all right? For god's sake speak, Mr Willmott! Oh dear, how pale you've gone!'

I will not enlarge on the painful scene that follows and which considerably increases Miss Lightbody's rather limited knowledge of diminutives, not to say the facts of life. Then comes her hurried telephone call to Wolverhampton, the immediate cancellation of SOD and the substitution of IMP ('They didn't sound very pleased and said could they have TIT instead but even I knew about that and so of course I said certainly not'). And so the busy day continues with a lot of worried head-shakings and discussions about BUB ('I do see what you mean, Tiny, but I truly think that that usage has long since dropped out') and a very firm line taken with the NE area who have had the effrontery to put in for SOW, NIT and GAY. It is of course important that an adjudicator should have a sound knowledge of most European languages. Although CON and CUL mean little or nothing to the average Englishman, the former word merely having about it an aura either of studious learning or of trickery, one has to bear in mind frog visitors to our shores who, hiring a car with such a number-plate, may consider themselves insulted. If you don't happen to know the meaning of CON in, say, Dieppe, I am certainly not going to enlighten you, and as for CUL, put on your thinking-caps, ponder on *cul-de-sac*, and work it out from there.

There are, of course, many borderline cases, as in the matter of BUB. Take the word URN which, when spoken, will remind admirers of Morecambe and Wise of the smaller one but which is basically a rather gloomy receptacle for ashes and is connected with bereavements and sombre attire and *visages*

*d'occasion.* Then one would hardly care to motor about labelled POX or PUS. The racially sensitive will have noticed that the word GOY is to be observed here and there but Mr Willmott has apparently not yet liberated JEW. I have still to see HUN and WET. It doesn't do to be too prissy and, although I myself do not greatly care for them, I truly cannot see anything fundamentally wrong with PEE and LOO, here together in what seems a sensible composite grouping, with one of them leading on, so to speak, to the other.

It is clear that sooner or later, and before the Labour Party starts playing Old Harry with established customs, the splendid Mr Willmott will qualify for, at least, an OBE and, delighted as one will be for him, I cannot imagine how the citation will read. 'For keeping our roads clean' might imply the head of a chain of dust-carts. 'For services to purity', perhaps. One can but wonder how the conversation would go at the Investiture. 'Congratulations, Mr Willmott. What is it that you do exactly?' 'I prevent the public being shocked by nasty little words on motor-cars, Ma'am.' 'Unacceptable graffiti, do you mean?' 'No, Ma'am. Registration words such as HAG, GUT and BOG.' 'Oh I see. Thank you. We are very pleased.'

# By your grace

I regret to have to report that I am one of those unsympathetic persons whose hearts sink down into their boots when somebody, brightly beaming, throws into our conversation the dreaded phrase 'I had ever such a funny dream last night.' How to stem the forthcoming torrent of words? There is usually nothing for it but to assume a pleased expression and absent the mind. Few dreams are very funny or interesting except to the dreamer. The recital of one is apt to kick off with daunting words such as 'I was in this strange car, you see . . .' or 'This extraordinary woman came up and said . . .' One knows the pattern all too well. And therefore it is with some diffidence and not without anxious wonderings that I here and now relate to you a dream I had. My excuse is that, as it concerns the very highest in the land, it is up to me, as a loyal subject, to keep you informed about life at Balmoral, where I usually meet her (breakfast on the terrace). It is alleged by trick-cyclists that to dream about the Queen is a clear proof that subconsciously one feels oneself to be socially inadequate. I hotly refute this. Nobody who knows and is chummy with my Devonian friends the Bultitudes can be considered in any way at all inadequate. Giles and Bunty are proof enough of my social security (in the non-financial sense), but if you require further reassurances, what about Canon Mountjoy, constantly at my table? What of my Cousin Madge? There you are, you see. My social life passes muster whichever way you care to turn.

However, it was indeed of Her Majesty that I dreamt though on this occasion we were not at Balmoral. Instead, Mahomet, so to speak, came to the mountain. I was at home and relaxing, having decided not to weed a rather unattractive section of a flower bed behind some fir trees, among the tasteful furnishings of my 'Myrtlebank' sitting-room (general colour scheme, apple green and yellow) when in she walked. No knock at the door or a warning cough or a polite 'Pardon me for intruding'. Just as bold as brass, if such a phrase doesn't smack of lèse-majesté, and wearing a fawn-coloured tailor-made. Not a great deal of jewellery and hatless, though usually she has got her crown on, even at breakfast (well, why not? If you've got it, wear it). She came straight to the point. 'Where's that reading list of books that I asked you to prepare for Prince Andrew?' I was, frankly, dumbfounded. When last we break-fasted together, about three months ago, our animated talk had not concerned books in any way but had been entirely about the difficulty of getting one's grocery and dairy purch-ases *out* of a supermarket (apparently she herself gets over this little trouble by just yelling 'I'm the Queen' and pushing her trolley straight through the cashier's check-out-point, a solu-tion not available to all). But books? One somehow doesn't picture any members of the royal family curled up with literature.

Playing frantically for time (she looked so dreadfully huffy and put out), I said that I hadn't yet had an opportunity of typing out the list but that I would gladly, and there and then, rattle off some names as they came to mind, upon which she let out a sound that would, in any of her subjects, be called quite simply a loud snort. However, I pressed on and we then moved into the world of Lewis Carroll. Playing for safety, the first title I suggested was *David Copperfield*. 'Piffle,' cried the Queen. What, then, about another treasure from our great national literary heritage, *The Light That Failed*? 'Bosh,' she shouted. *A Passage to India*, *Under the Greenwood Tree* and *Middle-march* were met with 'Rubbish,' 'Nonsense' and 'Worst book I ever read.' Stung by a particularly noisy shriek of 'Tripe!' when I rather daringly put forward the name of a personal favourite, *A Handful of Dust*, I plucked up my courage and said, rather severely, that it seemed to me a pity that she was being so unladylike. 'A Queen can't be a lady, and vice versa,' she said in a very snubbing manner and then vanished. I was far from displeased to see her go. Then I woke up, rather shaken. It was just after 5 a.m. and the birds were twittering and enjoying an early snack. I keep at the bedside, fearful of dehydration, a glass of orangeade covered with an old envelope in case a fly, blundering about by night, should find there a damp grave, and while I took a refreshing sip, I found myself pondering about what, these days, constitutes a lady.

Not so very long ago, the signs were many. She had servants. She wore, whenever possible, gloves. She went to church. She never in any circumstances raised her voice, no matter how trying the conditions (falling over a cliff). She had days, even up to the 1930s, when she was 'at home'. She ceaselessly wrote letters (it was very far from acceptable to do a lot of telephoning) in an enormous and flowing hand, about ten words to the page. She seemed not much to notice anything that was disturbing or in any way nasty (wasn't it dear Queen Alexandra who, motoring through some of the most appalling of the East End slums, used to keep up a monotonous rumble of 'Poor things, poor things'?). She drank a glass of madeira and ate a small piece of Dundee cake about 11 a.m. By the age of fifty she was more or less done for physically and retired to a sofa and rugs and embroidery and ear-trumpets. Oh yes, and she was rich too, or at least relatively so. The Victorians, who really invented 'the lady' and were quite desperately conscious of what constituted one and what didn't, wouldn't at all have approved of a lady being poor. But nowadays when everybody is poor, few attend church, gloves are rare, there are no ear-trumpets and if a lady retired to a sofa, she would have to get smartly off it again in order to go and fetch her lunch, what infallible signs are left to us? To whom can one turn for that really final and authoritative word on this difficult subject?

To help us in our enquiries, who better than the publishers who flourish beneath the name Debrett's Peerage Ltd, even though ladies are by no means only to be found in noble families ('and vice versa', as HM would undoubtedly quip). They have now encouraged Douglas Sutherland, who put us all straight on the subject of 'The English Gentleman', to tackle, at £3.50 a time, *The English Gentleman's Wife*, or lady. Debrett's, possibly out to dazzle dull old you and me, provide a foreword by a duchess, no less, and an introduction by Lady Windlesham, but after that, Mr Sutherland takes over and gets down to more ordinary and everyday matters. He it was, you recall, who fearlessly informed us in the previous volume that gentlemen simply do not live in Surrey and thereby caused consternation among the carports and barbecues and loggias of Guildford and Haslemere and Godalming. Maybe he is right. This was, after all, the area inhabited by Carl Peterson and Dr Lakington, and they don't come any more ungentlemanly than that. Even the future Mrs Bulldog Drummond's

*She never in any circumstances raised her voice, no matter how trying the conditions*

father, who lived there too, was a skilled forger, in the intervals of weaving his wobbly way to the sideboard to punish the whisky decanter yet again.

'Although times have changed, the female animal,' our duchess assures us, 'has not changed so very much,' but the young man of today, if he is after the best, must be quick off the mark ('young lovelies can be out of reach in no time'). Never mind. 'Rest assured, there are plenty of models, secretaries and yes, debutantes, for the less adventurous suitor.' Oh good. Boldly stating that 'any wife worth her keep can drive a horsebox', our noble informant then tugs aside the strawberry-leaves and allows us a peep at home life:

> Many years ago when I had a pack of hounds, I virtually had to resign the Mastership due to lack of a 'surrogate wife', as no one domestic servant today could ever be coerced into undertaking the duties expected of an English Gentleman's Wife. I needed a 'wife' to scrub the breeches, polish the boots, sew on the buttons, drive my daughters to school, answer the telephone, deal with the chicken claims, fetch the dead and rotting flesh for the kennels. Then, after all this, make herself charming to everyone at the meet and generally arrange a Master's social life. But at that time, good 'wives' seemed to be at a premium, and I couldn't get one for love or money, even when concealing the fact that I didn't propose giving much of either of those commodities to any prospective applicant.

I do see why nobody pressed forward.

# What a performance

It is not in my frivolous nature to look on the black side of things for very long, although there has recently, both in our own dishevelled land and elsewhere, been reason enough for acute glumness. But 'there's a silver lining' the poetess rightly informs us (in this case, Lena Guilbert Ford) 'through the dark cloud shining' and though her message was enshrined in a 1914 wartime injunction, made memorable by Ivor's music, to keep the home fires burning (till the boys come home) it holds good for other occasions and telly buffs will have grasped eagerly an unexpected 'repeat' treat, a silver lining indeed, provided one Saturday afternoon a week or so ago by the BBC. I am of course referring to the performance, in old-fashioned black-and-white though so vivid was it that it seemed to glow richly with colour, of that immensely tuneful and merry musical film, *Naughty Marietta*, starring chunky Nelson Eddy in full voice and somehow pleasingly reminiscent, so blond and baritoney, of Mr Heath, and the world's singing favourite, Jeanette MacDonald, every canine and incisor on view and a gleaming glittering advertisement for both Pepsodent and healthy living.

The film's lyrics, the tasteful work of Rita Johnson Young, contain what are my favourite five words assembled in poetic form. They are put, and confidently put, into the mouth of lovesick Mr Eddy as, alone in a boat with Miss MacDonald, they drift together down a river and down Love's Pathway too. Gazing at the radiant vision, all coy smiles and fragrant womanhood, before him, Mr Eddy inflates his lungs while the violins begin to scrape and, after preparing the ground with lesser words, boldly lets fly with the line 'My spirits are truly unruly', a statement which not only rhymes rather cleverly but which furnishes such a succinct summary of his throbbing emotions at the time. They don't for some reason make films like this any longer and more's the pity. A question hovers in the mind. For whom can the BBC intend these rather outmoded and esoteric filmic pleasures? Perhaps there are many more droopy old buffers like myself about than one imagines. If so, hooray.

A fondness for, and familiarity with, the altogether easier kinds of poetry has been with me since about the age of five. In what I see now to have been a disastrously encouraging educational programme, I was urged from a very early age, and by grown-ups who should have known better but who must have had some morbid kind of death wish, to get up and recite, and for recitations one required poetry. Nor was poetry all. I could manage worse than poetry. Individual singing was welcomed at my prep school, where the adults must also have been gluttons for punishment, and those of us who learnt the piano learnt also how to accompany ourselves, while vocally inspired, at the school upright. We practised, keen to show off, assiduously and every holiday I took home with me, so to speak, a freshly learnt song of the 'Early One Morning' or 'Funiculi Funicula' kind and, scarcely off the train and disentangled from my mother's embrace, I would move confidently to the Bechstein and give tongue in what was obviously a totally repellent manner. How appalled she must have been by this but, never one to be unkind or discouraging, she bore all stoically, though I do seem to remember her sometimes absenting herself and listening from another room ('I shall hear you perfectly, dear').

And now, impossible to shake off and firmly with one for what remains of life's journey, are the jolly jingles and the verse, good and bad, of childhood, the recitation pieces that sometimes found even the greatest of poets in less ponderous mood, almost playful even and with Alfred Lord Tennyson himself no exception. The first world war on the home front was a prime time for charity concerts and silver collections for service comfort funds, and a child reciter was, it seems, a pleasing and welcome spectacle, for how else to explain the fact that a small girl, Mary White, and I, both aged seven, were so much in demand at that time in the Barnes area? Learning by heart was no bother at all and we each had a small repertoire of acceptable poems. Mary's smash hit was 'Cradle Song', a charming lightweight from the said Laureate's pen and beginning with the line 'What does little birdie say in her nest at peep of day?' For those whose memory of the poem has become dimmed, let me explain that birdie wants, naturally, to fly away, a premature course of action wisely counselled against by the mother bird. 'Birdie' then gives place to 'baby', also wishful to run before it can walk, and with the same restraining result. It was a short poem and it always went to storms of applause but try as I may I could never get Mary to agree that the piece would gain even more in appeal if she would lisp it. 'What doth little birdie thay in her netht at peep of day?' would give the thing, though I didn't put it quite like that, an extra dimension. But my co-star was huffy. She didn't, she coldly explained, lisp – a feeble argument. Instinct told me that she was missing a fine chance here. And if she changed 'her' to 'his' she could get in another lisp (hith).

Never mind. Lisped or not, 'Cradle Song' was a safe starter for our section of the programme. When the last plaudits were dying away (Mary's mother, prominently placed in Row B, formed a valuable one-women claque) I assumed what I hoped was a pleasing and modest expression and, advancing to the front of the platform, let rip a blatant tear-jerker, Cibber's 'The Blind Boy'. When originally 'doing' this poem, a kind teacher had, with an eye to the dramatic effect, advised me to pretend to grope and stumble my way blindly forward and, while reciting, try to look sightlessly into the middle distance, but attempts to achieve this moving helplessness produced nothing but a rather tipsy walk coupled with such an appalling and alarming squint that the audience tittered uncontrollably, and it was certainly not titters that I was after. I soon abandoned such risky procedures and just closed my eyes in a sympathetic manner. From the very first line – 'O say what is this thing call'd Light?', a respectful silence fell, for the hospitals of nearby Roehampton were no strangers to blinded soldiers, parties of whom could be seen occasionally sunning themselves on Barnes Common. And then, in happier vein, Mary and I joined forces for Kipling's 'Where are you going to all you big steamers?', a tactful tribute to our gallant navies, merchant and otherwise, with Mary posing the various questions and looking wistful but with not, little fool, a lisp in her, and me providing the hearty and reassuring answers, hitching up my bags and every inch the jolly jack tar. When I say that for the concert I appeared, as did many young children in those days, in a sailor suit, the entirely repulsive nature of my contribution will be apparent. Tea with the mayor or his representative, and sometimes a present of chocs, closed the afternoon. The conception that the entertainment had ever been anything but perfectly executed never once crossed my sadly confident little mind.

And then in my first year at Oundle there was again nothing but encouragement to be poetically up and doing. First year boys took part in a class called 'Repetition' on the stage of the school hall. This involved acting scenes from Shakespeare and elsewhere, but with a novel approach. Everybody had to join in, irrespective of the size of the cast and so there would be eight Hamlets speaking in unison and three Ophelias and six Horatios and two (quite enough) Gertrudes. Five Shylocks found themselves being looked straight in the eye by nine Portias. This method encouraged the faint-hearted and shed the dramatic load. It also allowed everybody to tread the boards in an important role. A splendid idea. What other school would ever have thought of *that*?

# Too bad to last

Lord Boothby, never one to stint the decibels when making a firm public pronouncement and for so long a warm, hilarious, informative and supremely non-boring feature of *Any Questions?*, has stated that in the Twenties he and his privileged friends and contemporaries, awash with pink champagne and busily engaged on all the pastimes that in that bizarre and restless period (should they be the Twitching Twenties?) were considered pleasurable – for some it meant parties in mews, tango teas, Charlestoning at Ciro's and punting with Phyllis to Boulter's Lock – used to greet each day with a cry of 'By God, this is far too good to last!' True in a sense, though for the socially secure and reasonably rich it lasted far longer than was either acceptable or expected, well into the Thirties in fact and surviving a general strike and a national government. And then with the jolt of the Abdication it was all over.

The leisured life that some enjoyed is amply stored away on fiction's pages, though it was far from fictional. If you remove the splendid jokes, the daily existence of Bertie Wooster and Jeeves would not have seemed at all unusual. Hugh Drummond, facing another idle day, would emerge from Half Moon Street and stroll (he never walked) in the sunshine up Piccadilly (getting a wave, one hopes, from Hugh Walpole in that first-floor flat on the corner: bulldogs were just his type). He was, of course, on his way to the Junior Sports' Club and beer and lunch with Archie Longworth and some rather less splendid jokes. Further down Piccadilly were to be found Lord Peter Wimsey and his servant, Bunter, cracking *their* jokes.

Indeed, apart from Wodehouse, the humour of the time was generally of a particularly trying kind, full of banter and badinage and nowhere more typical than in the occasional domestic pieces that A. A. Milne supplied to humorous journals and which were greatly relished in the Twenties. A reassuring and affluent note was struck from the first ('We gathered round the billiard-room fire') and the girls were from the same stable as Sapper's 'topping fillies' and tended to be called Myra or Dahlia or Celia. The pieces usually began with some such phrase as 'It was all Celia's fault' and went on to describe some amusing mishap in the home, perhaps an inexperienced parlourmaid getting into a muddle with unfamiliar finger-bowls and solemnly putting out towels and soap as well. Killing.

It is quaint that names should have been considered such a fine subject for laughter. Mr Milne tells of a parrot called Evangeline, suggests names for a new-born baby (Montmorency Plantagenet), calls his clocks after the kind of people who gave them to him (Enid, Percy and Alphonse), requests his housekeeper to look after a newly-acquired Japanese dwarf-tree ('Let me introduce you to Sidney') and is in no doubt at all about what to call imaginary gentlemen involved in financial dealings in the City (Sir Isaac Isaacstein and Sir Moses Mosesstein). Names are a fearful trap. Even when the dazzling *No No Nanette* burst on us in the mid-Twenties (as big a musical play breakthrough in its time as *Oklahoma*), one saw with gloom that in the cast list, 'Lucille's friends' who join her, as you'll recall, at The Cottage, Sunnycliff in Act II, had all been given supposedly rich married status (Mrs Smythe-Smith, Mrs Goring-Jones and so on). There has never been anything remotely funny about made-up double-barrelled names (the real ones are another matter). The relative lack of real humour in the Twenties is both puzzling and regrettable. Nobody even gave a half-smile when bold Iris Storm in *The Green Hat* said 'I am a house of men' or when D. H. Lawrence, not the loudest giggler in the class, wrote in all seriousness after milking a cow: 'The queer cowy mystery of her is her changeless cowy desirableness.' How profound, everybody thought.

It is usually better for historians to stand back and remain remote from the events they chronicle but the most effective writers on the Twenties are those who lived through them and experienced for themselves the strange and rather feverish feel in the air. The best record I know, of the lighter kind, is Beverley Nichols's *The Sweet and Twenties*, written, with both affection and amazement, about 30 years after that weird decade. Here's a feast of recall! Famous women had not yet learnt to beware of journalists and gladly sounded off on a number of subjects, with even Queen Marie of Roumania chatting away about life ('I, for one, like a man to be a man') together with Elinor Glyn ('Tell your readers that sex has never touched the hem of my garment'). 'Tumbril talk' was everywhere, Mrs Ronald Greville, the busiest of hostesses, wailing 'One uses up *so* many red carpets in a season' and announcing that she always carried 'a little loose change' in her bag (it turned out to be a sum of about £600).

Mild eccentrics flourished: Lord Berners had a small piano built into his Rolls-Royce and Max Beerbohm asserted that the only really satisfactory place in London for a writer to work in was the Charing Cross Hotel. When Lord Alington accused Michael Arlen of wearing a made-up bow tie, they scuffled excitingly on the steps of White's Club. Meanwhile *The Times* was attacking Epstein ('We feel a bewilderment . . .'), the wireless arrived, and there was a fine old fussification over poor Radclyffe Hall (the writer and not an Oxford College) and her very mildly homosexual book, *The Well of Loneliness*, about which James Douglas, the Mrs Whitehouse of the Twenties, nearly had a seizure. Shingled or Eton-cropped women smoked Russian cigarettes in long holders. Red leather HMV portables ground out 'novelty piano solos' such as 'Kitten on the Keys', everybody hooted at Mrs Baldwin's ghastly hats, and cook-generals were lucky if they got £1 a week.

It is understandable that Sandy Wilson, born in 1924 but responsible with *The Boy Friend* for one of the brightest and most characteristic period musical comedies, should have been tempted, in *The Roaring Twenties* (Eyre Methuen: £2.50), to have a go at resuscitating some of the peculiarities and, lacking personal adult experience, he has wisely kept the text to a minimum and concentrated on pictorial illustration. Again, what a feast. Jaunty Anita Loos in a cloche hat, Hollywood 'orgy' scenes from Elinor Glyn's *Three Weeks* (no orgies were considered complete without a bowl of rather squashy dark blue grapes), Marie Stopes victimised for her progressive views, flappers enjoying the 'flapper vote' of 1929 with all the bystanders in stitches, Josephine Baker wearing a girdle of diamanté bananas, the Astaires, Noël and Gertie . . . Lovely for some.

# Hip hip hurrah

'Where's the happy little sand-boy that I used to know?' a wonky master at my preparatory school once wistfully asked me in a week when I was looking, for a change, sad and moody. It was in December 1923 and the incident is, like so many in childhood, still perfectly clear to me. I was emotionally much cast down by the death, at the age of 24, of an actress of brilliant promise called Meggie Albanesi, news of which had just reached me via the *Daily Mail*, a newspaper taken for us because it contained a popular comic strip featuring a mouse called Teddy Tail. Miss Albanesi was extremely highly rated by both critics and the public and there is a bust of her in the St Martin's Theatre (you can take in *The Mousetrap* at the same time). 1923 had anyhow been theatrically a disastrous year, for in March Sarah Bernhardt had gone, and she I felt to be almost a personal friend, having seen her a few years before in a dramatic sketch at the Coliseum, even though it was more or less by mistake (we had gone to enjoy a famous troop of Chinese acrobats, who all stood on top of each other). But there she was, an old lady with frizzy hair lying on a sofa and gabbling incomprehensibly. I think it must have been a war-time 'charity performance' in aid of wounded soldiers and the Red Cross. It was not at the time apparent that she had only one leg, and I am sorry to report that one longed for her to shut up so that we could get to the tumblers.

By the age of ten I knew, such was my keenness, the names of every leading performer on the English stage, and a number of foreigners besides, together with a good deal of fancy, and doubtless invented, stuff about what seemed to be their enchanting private lives, dished up attractively with photographs in the weekly *Sketch* and *Bystander* ('By the by, buy the *Bystander*' the advertisements encouraged). So, despite these shattering deaths, I cheered up fairly sharply by thinking of

Phyllis Dare and Charles Hawtrey and Beatrice Lillie and soon regained my sand-boy status, upon which, I regret to say, the schoolmaster became a good bit less wistful and more practical in his attentions.

When not happily in a theatre, my spare time was spent 'devouring', as they say, theatrical information and literature of every kind. The appallingly precarious nature of the profession was made known to all by the amounts of money that some theatre people left. There was the hugely successful Oscar Asche who wrote, and acted in, the record-breaking *Chu-Chin-Chow* and who departed this life a mere £20 to the good. There was Nijinsky (dotty, and £31). W. Graham Browne, Marie Tempest's husband, scraped together £441. Poor Davy Burnaby, the genial chairman of the unforgettable *Co-optimists*, only rang the bell at £21. One longed to know more about the actual acting but, even when I was young, the biographies and autobiographies of the great seemed to me poorly done, and I now realise that there are few things harder to write. One learned so little of value: it was all largely domestic tosh.

Every now and then, however, there were helpful hints to be garnered. To the New Theatre, Cambridge, there came in the late 1920s the famous theatrical touring company of Sir Frank Benson, mobile nursery of so many fine players and specialising in the plays of Shakespeare (apart from anything else, no author's percentage to have to shell out). Sir Frank was indeed, to borrow Miss Gingold's description of the late Sir Donald Wolfit, a *force de tour*. He seemed to us undergraduates unbelievably ancient and I see now that, born in 1858, he must have been 70. This did not prevent him, game to the last, from playing Hamlet.

In black tights and tottering about fencing with Laertes, he made a most alarming spectacle and one had to avert one's gaze from his shrunk shanks. His youthful mother, Gertrude, looked like his grand-daughter. It was all rather sad and muddling but about a year later he vouchsafed to the world in book form some of the strange secrets of his baffling art, together with tips about how to get on. I have the book still. Breathe deeply 'through eyes, ears, mouth, nose and chin', he counsels. Keep quite tremendously 'fit', like Ellen Terry ('I have seen her spring at the connecting rod between two pieces of scenery as it was being raised to the flies and be whisked up

*One had to avert one's gaze from his shrunk shanks*

thirty or forty feet, laughing and singing'). Form a rugger team from the company and issue challenges to local sides ('Oh look, Macbeth has scored a try!'). Keep a straight left ready for insults ('Near the Lyceum, a drunkard hissed the words "Bloody aesthete!"'). To assist lissomness, 'practise Chinese sideways kicks with the knee joints flexible'. Sir Frank adds, *à propos de* not very much, that 'next to actors, the lives of country clergy rank highest for insurance purposes'. But of course: the risk of assassination in the vestry following an hour-long sermon, or a nasty tumble down the chancel steps after too conscientiously making sure that the communion wine is at room temperature.

It is left, however, to Mme Bernhardt herself, to bring us in *My Double Life* (1907 originally, but now reissued by Peter Owen at £6.95) the liveliest of theatrical memoirs of the fairly distant past. Though physically unsuitable in some ways, being slender as a needle in those days of bulging bosoms, and with 'hair as curly as a white negress', she had nevertheless the long arms necessary for expansive gestures (you can't get through Racine without them), a magical voice, and the will to win. She is pleasingly truthful about her beginnings and set-backs – second prize only for tragedy at the Conservatoire and in 1862 her début at the Comédie was 'a complete failure'.

It is quite clear from those who saw her in her prime, Maurice Baring among them, that for dramatic talent she was a total knockout and before very long what we have to refer to as *tout-Paris* was at her gifted feet. 'Hip-hip-hurrah!' they kept going (alas, the name of the original English translator is denied us but here's a greeting to him or her across the years). She cleverly managed to arrange that her so-called private life was no less interesting than her public one. In due course, a male child, source unrevealed, popped out. She took to sleeping in her coffin. She was ever ready to slap a face or to fall senseless to the floor ('I decided therefore to faint'). Wherever she went, she saw to it that 'gossip with its thistle-down wings took flight in all directions'. She met Victor Hugo ('so witty and refined') and was a pioneer in the field of trips by balloon, entering the basket with foie gras, champagne and Prince Jerome Napoleon ('Plon-plon' to close friends) and keeping a firm hand on the controls when the time came to descend ('Kindly open the valve').

She stormed London, the actual storming ('Hip-hip-hurrah!') beginning as far away as Folkestone where Forbes Robertson handed her a gardenia, a crowd of thousands shouted '*Vive* Sarah Bernhardt!' and an armful of lilies and the loudest hip-hip of all came from 'a turbulent young man with luminous eyes and long hair' called Oscar Wilde. Henry Irving provided a bouquet and muted hurrahs. Then, after a triumphant success, and clutching, for one never knew, 'a very prettily chased revolver, ornamented with cats-eyes', she stormed America ('Hip-hip-hurrah for Sarah Bernhardt!'). Here, despite 'unspeakably awful food', there were fresh triumphs and a heart-warming incident. During a gala performance of *La Dame aux Camélias* and just when Marguerite Gautier has seated her guests at the supper table, the entire scenery collapsed on them and their heads, perforating the thin canvas, were held immobile and sticking up out of the debris. Very few star performers would relate such an undignified disaster, let alone find it hilarious. Hip-hip-hurrah indeed.

# Mind your own business

'O fat white woman' runs the poem, 'whom nobody loves, why do you walk through the fields in gloves, missing so much and so much?' It has always seemed to me somewhat impertinent of Frances Cornford, though a gifted poetess and a delightful person in other ways, to have assumed, without supporting evidence of any kind, that 'nobody loves' the fat white lady, a politer word than 'woman', whom she saw, as we recall, from a train and who, strolling through the fields, happened to be wearing gloves (possibly a sensible precaution against midge bites). In my mind's eye I see the well known and widely anthologised event taking place on a Sunday morning in summer on a branch railway line somewhere in Cambridgeshire. The three-carriage local train, its engine puffing steam, chugs clanking round a bend and there, on one of the flat and soggy meadows for which that rather unlovely county is famous, can be seen a white and obese female figure sturdily making her way through the cowslips, the cow parsley, the cowpats, and, *ergo*, cows.

I do not understand why Mrs Cornford, comfortably settled in a window seat of a third class non-smoker, should have taken quite such as instant dislike to her. It was almost certainly the vicar's wife, released from the Matins for which she would naturally have donned gloves and off on an errand of mercy before lunch (blanket bath for poor old bedridden Mrs Merryweather). As a general rule, plump persons are jollier than skinny ones (well, take a look round your chums). Why not 'fat white woman whom *everyone* loves'? Perhaps Mrs Cornford had gulped her breakfast, now had indigestion and wanted to take the unpleasant pains out on somebody. There is another problem, the word 'white'. Was she wearing white, or had she a reddish face that she had conscientiously powdered down for church? Was the train passing through a

*It was almost certainly the vicar's wife*

predominately West Indian district and therefore a white woman was a rarity? We shall, I expect, in due course know the full circumstances. Who can doubt that somewhere in an American university, a diligent Eng. Lit. student with a half completed Cornford thesis is at this very moment struggling to identify the gloved stranger?

Impertinence, idiotic statements and stupid queries are, in the literary world, by no means confined to poetesses. Could any question possibly be more ill-judged than, in Isaiah, the cry of 'Watchman, what of the night?' The watchman, appointed by the Lord himself at an undisclosed salary but thought to be in the region of £22 a week with supper vouchers, has already, peering into the darkness with his eyes peeled, observed a two-horse chariot, a number of asses and camels, and just the one lion. What a moment for distracting him with a request for a weather forecast and time check, and indeed, all that the watchman can politely gasp out, probably wondering whether the lion has recently eaten, is that at some time or other it will be morning again, followed later on by another night, facts which were already plain to all.

Occasionally of course a poet provides a perfectly legitimate question. The ghost who materialises himself to an outwardly calm A. E. Housman and asks 'Is my team ploughing?' is, obviously, anxious for up-to-the-minute agricultural news from leafy Shropshire. The reference to 'team', hotly followed by a request for information about the local football XI and how they are making out on that rather bumpy river-side pitch, has led to confusion. Let me clarify. 'Team' here refers to horses. Footer involves, I am afraid, 'lads', a description that is sometimes, and in some mouths, a bit of a give-away, and here we have the word five times in eight verses. It always put Maurice Bowra on his guard ('Whenever I hear that unfortunate word 'lad', I sniff about for something discreditable').

In the field of tactlessness, Sir John Suckling's questions ('Why so pale and wan?') to a lovesick young man who is making no headway ('Why so dull and mute?') with his Miss Right, are extremely out of place. Whatever J. Suckling was knighted for, it can hardly have been *savoir-faire*. And about the poet Thomas Dekker, evil exploiter of a grossly underpaid labour-force, NS readers will naturally wish me to speak very sharply. It was, admittedly, in 1632 but it's never too late to right a wrong. It is not quite clear exactly what the labour-force was labouring at. Can Dekker possibly be an early form of Decker and they were forerunners of the admirable firm of Black & Decker and were therefore manufacturing a primitive form of water-driven power tool? No matter, whatever it was and to keep them quiet, hateful and unscrupulous Dekker ceaselessly fed them with blatantly false information. He kicks off strongly. 'Art thou poor, yet has thou golden slumbers?' he cries. Rubbish! Poverty means hunger, and hunger means empty stomachs, and empty stomachs produce ear-splitting rumbles and render slumber, golden or otherwise, out of the question for all but the stone-deaf. Briskly painting an entirely false picture of the horrors of being rich, and certain that he has now duped his hearers, he presses on with his real message, which is 'Work apace, apace, apace, apace', adding, as though it were some sort of comfort, 'Honest labour bears a lovely face.' We could all take him to some areas where it does no such thing. And then, abandoning all pretence, one can see him going skipping down the street on his way to the Boar's Head and a double sack with an almost unbelievably heartless cry of 'Then hey nonny nonny – hey nonny nonny!' Verse 2 is even more disgracefully misleading – the benefits of drinking water, the glory of enduring want, the deeply sad life of the wealthy, further cries of 'work apace', and more unbridled and delirious hey nonny nonnies all the way to the bank.

In the field of unreliability, unbalanced judgments and impertinent behaviour, there is nobody more hoity-toity and unsatisfactory than Wordsworth. I can hardly think that education at St John's College, Cambridge was responsible for such airs and graces. One is doubtful from the first. Anybody who can think so highly of the cuckoo ('Thrice welcome, darling of the spring!'), a deeply unattractive and morally depraved bird if ever there was one, is immediately suspect. And then, on a trip to Scotland he arrives at the charmingly demure little town of Yarrow in Selkirk, and what do we find: 'And is this – Yarrow? *This*?' The italics are the poet's own and especially offensive to the inhabitants. His fellow visitors to Selkirk fare as badly ('These tourists, Heaven preserve us, needs must live'). Travelling abroad is one long round of complaint ('A plague on your languages, German and Norse') and there was a singularly ill-informed view of the French revolution – 'Oh! pleasant exercise of hope and joy', and such cheery news to receive in the tumbril. No attempt is made to disguise grumpy moods ('Oh for a dirge!') and he is inconsiderate to a degree when, wishful for a companion for a slog over the fells, he bursts in on a crony deep in the latest thriller from Mudie's with a shout of 'Up! up! my friend and quit your books.' In all, a sorry record. I do not read modern poets because I can so seldom understand what they are talking about. But I bet they are a lot nicer. 'Scorn not the Sonnet' wails Wordsworth. But that's exactly what I plan to do.

# See how they run

Schoolmasters everywhere, either still serving or, like myself, now liberated from the classroom and rusting away in wheezy retirement, will have been completely aghast at a recent scholastic announcement in the *Daily Telegraph* and, for all I know, *The Times* as well. It concerned Rugby School and I italicise its alarming feature. 'The school will disperse' it said, more or less, 'for the Easter holidays on 26 March *and the Crick will be run on the same day.*' To refresh my memory of the Crick, the famous Rugby competitive run, I naturally flew to my copy of *Great Public Schools* (1890). Just as I thought. The runners leave the main school buildings and thud along roads and footpaths to Crick village, and then thud back via Hillmorton, a distance of about 12 miles which a well-nourished schoolboy in good health should be able to complete in about an hour and a half.

School special trains always leave, as everybody knows, at 7 a.m. By 6.45 a.m. the entire place is virtually deserted. This must surely mean therefore that, to allow the runners time for a tosh (bath) afterwards, together with breakfast, presentation of prizes, awarding of athletic colours, severe censure of those who have done badly, etc., the Crick must be started in almost total darkness (my diary shows that moonlight on 26 March will be of negligible assistance) at not a moment later than 3.50 a.m. Such violent exertion in the small hours may well be injurious to health. Has the opinion of the school doctor been sought? Have the parents of the youthful competitors been consulted? And here there is too a serious moral risk, the temptation to take short cuts and, hidden by the dark mantle of night, miss out Crick altogether. A thoughtful word from the school chaplain just before the 'off' might be helpful, but possibly only those boys whose moral fibre has been strengthened by confirmation should be allowed to compete. The whole event bristles, as you see, with problems.

I can only hope that Rugby's unwise action will not set a perilous precedent, for there are many other school 'runs' to consider. At Malvern, not a school to encourage molly-coddles, they run up a mini-mountain, a risky undertaking at night. Then what of Loretto's Long Wallyford, Repton's Short Milton and, in the centre of Cambridge, the Klondyke run at The Leys which, a relatively recent foundation, will certainly not want a percentage of its more athletic boys squashed flat in the darkness by jumbo lorries. At Oundle we had the Cotter-stock which one year was enlivened by a very flamboyant schoolboy called Gabriel Toyne, who had managed to get himself into the *Public-Schools' Book of Verse* with a poem called 'Ode to a nymph with hands held cup-wise o'er a well' and who later became, suitably enough, an actor. Breasting the tape at the end of Cotterstock, arms flung wide, he gave a loud shriek, collapsed in a heap and fainted dead away. We gathered round. 'Tell me,' he gasped on recovering, 'tell me, did I win?' 'Well, not exactly,' we said. 'Actually, you came in 31st.'

Alongside *Great Public Schools* there sits on my shelves another invaluable volume which acts as a companion to it, namely *The Public School Word-Book* (1900), a handy glossary of words and phrases in use at those currently despised establishments. Those who disapprove of public schools may get what comfort they can from the assurance that examination of their past history reveals nothing but spartan living, extremely hard work, minimal amounts of food and regular beatings. Envious working lads, totally misled by Frank Richards, who had never been to a public school, and the fictional extravagances and merry jollities of 'Greyfriars', might well have found themselves wishing to return home to mum.

And it was no good complaining. Mutinous fags at Rugby were thrashed with three ash saplings, the idea being that the thrashing was to continue until two of the saplings had broken. At Winchester they popped them into a pillory and then lashed away with apple twigs. Tonbridge used the cane and further north they favoured a tanned leather strap called a tawse. Schoolmasters were known as bum-brushers and creature comforts were few. The boiled beef at Shrewsbury was sufficiently disgusting to cause a school uprising, the whole of the sixth form being subsequently expelled.

The *Word-Book* throws up some fine oddities, Winchester being particularly fruitful. Saintly junior boys at Stonyhurst, invited to attend 'The Resurrection' at 6 p.m. may well have wondered what new religious excitement was about to burst on the world and felt justifiably let down on finding themselves merely permitted to gobble up the dry remains of a speech-day beano. Here and there are a number of school words that knowledgeable, worldly and, I am sorry to say, coarse-minded persons may think that they already know. But they don't. Thus we find clap (to push in front of others at Christ's Hospital), charlies (thick Winchester gloves made of twine), schitt (a goal at football), tits (students at Durham University), cocks (the old washing place at Charterhouse), wanker (a bloater at Felsted), privates (private lessons at Harrow), old bag (stale milk at Westminster), short behind (half-back at Eton), tart-feast (end of term festivity at Stonyhurst), continent (to be ill at Winchester), and Matron's-gift (a rather nasty cream cheese at Christ's Hospital).

If, at Winchester, you wished to prop up a piece of furniture with a wedge under the leg, there was a verb to help you (to poon). The general absence of nourishment, with plain bread ('toak' at Repton) for breakfast, caused a lively interest in eggs and to show ostentatious zeal at Marlborough was 'to egg-up'. The Founder's Commemoration Day at Winchester was keenly awaited and called 'egg-flip day', cupfuls of the deliciousness being then served to all. Felsted seems to have had an almost incomprehensible custom concerning eggs. 'A boy seen carrying an egg or eggs, if addressed by another as "EGGOTTY", might, must in fact, almost in honour, throw an egg at him. If the egg-owner was a good shot, he would invite his friend to "call me EGGOTTY".' Oh I say, thanks awfully.

Etonian words, half heard and misremembered down the years, are a baffling lot. What can it mean to be 'up to Lyttelton on Lower Tuppeny', if I've got it right? And there is another phrase, evidently indicating excellence – to be 'sent up for good'. Odd that elsewhere this would mean that a la-di-da deviate was being permanently exposed to ridicule.

But the words had their uses. The odd public school names were able to trip up the bogus Tichborne claimant. Asked what 'bandy' meant at Stonyhurst, he said at first that it was a nickname, changing this subsequently to 'part of the college buildings'. It is neither, but a primitive form of Stonyhurst hockey. So sucks!

# May it please your majesty

Oundle, of which, as you know, I happily write from time to time, was a name that, though well enough known, and deservedly so, in the better educational circles, was some fifty years ago not at all familiar to the world at large. Even its pronunciation was to some a bit of a puzzle (it is pronounced not as in 'Oooh!' but as in 'Ow!' Boys with even the faintest suspicion of a Cockney accent were encouraged to think of it as 'Arndle'). The unfamiliarity meant that the name got itself quite often quaintly transformed. If you wrote that 'O' with the slightest of wobbles, and the rest of it not very distinctly, you were in trouble at once. Writing to London for Gamage's catalogue, that prime pre-Christmas treat, or to Gertrude Lawrence, a treat all the year round, for a photograph, the answer sometimes came back addressed to A. Marshall, Dugden House, Bundle, near Peterborough. Bundle alternated with Durdle, a name by which the place is still affectionately known to many ex-inmates. Occasionally Oundle became Dundee and Miss Lawrence had quite a nice little round trip.

And speaking of names, I am afraid that in some, if not all, ways this column must be an unrewarding disappointment to many of my readers. No exalted and ritzy social doings. No thrilling political experiences (brunch with the Healeys). No rich names in rich places. No chatterbangs with the eminent. It is, instead, a muted record of a life of all-round failure but I have always set my face against making an attempt to jolly up my thin material in the way that gossip writers do by placing key names in heavy black bold letters which then leap excitingly out at you from the text. It would be simplicity itself to give a wildly false impression of the peaceful daily round at Appleton by writing: 'Went to the village and bought some **Rolls**, wishing that I were the **Aga Khan** and could afford to do all my shopping at **Harrods**. At the travelling library, searched in vain for a life of **Princess Grace of Monaco** but had to settle instead for the latest **Daphne du Maurier.** Then home through the orchard, reminding myself that the **Duke of Devonshire,** which fruited so finely last year, requires a good mulch. Opened a tin of baked beans, placed them on buttered toast and then munched my lunch, listening to **Beethoven** on Radio 3 and wondering what **The Queen** was having for *her* lunch.'

Actually, we no longer need to be in doubt about any detail of her day by day life for the indefatigable Helen Cathcart has been, in *The Queen in Her Circle*, at it again. Mrs Cathcart, a reverential curtsey in every line of her rich prose, has already covered (an unfortunate verb, perhaps, in that hugely horse-infested world) the Queen Mother, and in rightly adulatory phrases but which remind one of giant dollops of sacchariney meringue, together with Princess Margaret, Prince Charles, Princess Anne, Lord Snowdon ('etc., etc.' boasts the book's list of this authoress's previous offerings, and who on earth can these nameless royal etceteras be?). W. H. Allen will sell you this latest work for £4.95, pleasing snaps and all.

We kick off in the Queen's sitting-room at Buckingham Palace, a retreat sourly described by Richard Crossman, our late editor and seldom given to looking on the bright side of things, as 'a dim, horrible little room'. Not too dusty, some might think: pale gold Chinese carpet, elephant-grey curtains, Waterford chandelier, and a profusion of what Mrs C, in a style all her own, insists on referring to as 'personal accessories', in this case mainly equestrian ones – bookends featuring Ascot postilions clip-clopping past the stands, a mounted guardsman in silver, racing trophies, a painting of the great winner, Aureole, and a porcelain model of Princess Anne clearing a fence (on a horse, of course), just a few of 'the remindful tokens that everywhere surround the Queen', plus a number of home-made calendars from 'the small fry who thus solve their Christmas gift problem for Aunt Lilibet'.

So serene is our chronicler's approach and her contented acceptance of what she finds, that one could easily imagine her fully at home even if wafted back about 440 years and into the reign of Henry VIII, himself no stranger, God knows, to personal accessories. 'His Majesty, in great heart and just home from hawking at Hounslow, let it be known amongst his closest circle that yet another of Dan Cupid's arrows had managed to pierce its way through our beloved monarch's

30

royal hauberk, this time in the personable person of a fair jewel from the august house of Howard. Methinks I hear wedding bells.' It seems possible that Henry VIII, who could stand just so much and was a person of, in some ways, considerable taste, might well have cooled off this well-intentioned writer in the Tower and confiscated her quill. No such luck nowadays.

On we press with our peep behind the scenes, delighted to find a sovereign who is pleasingly animated when off duty, 'eyes sparkling, hands waving, voice bubbling, nicknames flying, full of fun and repartee, a raconteur'. Just like you and me, you see, and never more so than when setting foot in downpours of rain, the first royal ruler since King John to do so, on Magna Carta Island in the Thames and being welcomed indoors by a couple who lived there ('Oh, Lord, my umbrella's dripped on your carpet'). However, it made, we are told, 'a fun day' and the Queen 'obviously enjoys extracting her own nuggets of experience'. And in case you should imagine, as so many did, that one of the nuggets was unacceptable and, at Princess Margaret's wedding, that was a disapproving face that Her Majesty had on, Mrs Cathcart has news for us. 'She was struggling to control her tender sentiment for her sister.' Oh I *see*. But of course!

Back we flash to long ago and the start of it all in 1923 ('Amid the potted palms and roses, Bertie and Elizabeth waltzed and foxtrotted'), and their first house, White Lodge in Richmond Park, with its mahogany-seated and throne-like lavatories and the Prince of Wales's ready wit ('They enjoyed his sally that the house was most commodious'). Then the arrival of Baby, dosed with dill-water to help it preserve a suitably relaxed demeanour for the christening photos, and the nanny, Alah, and the governess, 'Crawfie' (what a scream it was when she sat down on a rickety gold chair in the Belgian Suite and went right through to the floor. We all *roared*), and then, of course, Margaret, individual as ever even when urgently summoned to the wartime air-raid shelter ('She wasted time in searching for a pair of the right-coloured knickers').

I do see that it is extremely difficult to write acceptably about living royalty but intending biographers should really think twice before they enshrine in mush a family which works so hard and with an efficiency that deserves better treatment. To love and admire is not enough. And alas, historians a hundred years hence, hunting about, hot for interesting certainties in the available material, will find such books about as valuable as bus tickets.

# In the picture

Kind readers of this column can hardly fail to have been impressed, as month succeeds to month, by the unusually wide sweep of my interests – teeth, God, kipper mousse, my Cousin Madge, Mozart's life in the hereafter, Boots' 'perfume counter', etc. etc. So I trust that I shall not be thought too philistine and indifferent to culture if I announce that I refuse to be bludgeoned into a state of panic by the newspapers over the fact that a picture by Gainsborough may be going to leave us.

The BBC provided a telly shot of the picture in question – a genial and prosperous brewer in rural surroundings. I have never seen the picture in person and rather doubt whether our paths will now ever cross. I face the prospect with fortitude. How long ago was it that we were all nudged into a condition of feverish anxiety over some canvas or other, the work of a continental, I fancy, that was allegedly at risk? We all eagerly and dutifully subscribed our 50p (or was it the ten bob era?) to keep it here. The artist's name, the picture, its subject and its date have all long since been wiped from memory's slate. Nor am I sure if we eventually stumped up enough cash to prevent the thing from leaving us. I hold the view that we have quite enough pictures. Too many, in fact. It wouldn't hurt us to let a few more go abroad. They will be treasured there far more lovingly than here.

It is mainly foreigners, not I, who daily fill the National Gallery. Passing the crowds jostling their way up its steps, it is phrases such as '*Aber, wo ist Elsa?*' and '*Dépêche-toi, Marie!*' that you hear, rather than 'We seem to have lost your mother.'

I regret the fact that the day of the Victorian 'picture that tells a story' is over. These artistic delights once proliferated and, gazed at in later years, sometimes provide simple pleasures not intended by the artist. It is some time since I saw a reproduction of the famous 'Sentence of Death'. As far as I recall, the master of the house has not been feeling quite up to the mark, internal twinges and so on, and has called in their trusty GP, dear old Doctor Boddington, who, prodding and peering and tapping and trying not to whistle under his breath, has sadly pronounced a terminal illness. There the stricken family sits, almost photographically reproduced in oil, digesting the unwelcome tidings. Nothing whatever to smile at here. Sometimes, when the story was a trifle obscure and the reasons for the tear-drenched faces a little puzzling, the picture became a 'problem picture', a subject for lively discussion over dinner.

Paintings of this sort might give new life to the Royal Academy. Of what might a modern story-cum-problem picture consist? I imagine one called, quite simply, 'Caught!', revealing a sunny shopping precinct somewhere in the Midlands, the Co-op window gleaming invitingly in the foreground and displaying notices announcing the day's most attractive and mouth-watering bargains (4p off baked beans, and tinned ravioli slashed to the bare minimum), with the local Tesco just visible, jammed to the doors and smiling a welcome, away on our right. A smartly turned out operative (a builder? A water board employee? A refuse collector?) is emerging from the nearby betting shop, his face just one big question mark. He is staring at his wife, a blindingly blonde housewife, snug in a suede coatee with chunky-knit dolman sleeves and nigger accessories, clip-clopping along the the pavement across the road. What is she up to? She has sailed straight past the laundrette, the alleged purpose of her outing, and is making her way instead into the Odeon, a building now mainly devoted to the numerical excitements of Bingo. But see, she has spotted her husband, realises that she has indeed been 'caught' and, with her face half turned, is angrily shouting something challenging at him. Her pouting, lipsticked mouth seems to be forming, so skilful is the painter and so bright his colours, the letter 'F'. 'Fancy seeing you!' perhaps, or 'Fred, but what a lovely surprise!' Anyway, whatever it is, the vivid figures and the rich background of commerce allied to pleasure, could form a charming picture of a bustling nation going splendidly about its business and luxuriating in the full lives that so many of us are now privileged to lead. The only 'problem' is what will occur when Len and Doreen get home.

There was a Victorian picture a century or so ago on another and, in this case, a slightly more unsettling domestic matter – a thrillingly dramatic but untitled marital confrontation from the extremely competent palette of Augustus Egg. The scene is set in a comfortable sitting-room interior, the elaborate gas chandelier and various sumptuous furnishings placing the family firmly in the £1,000 p.a. bracket (three indoor servants and holidays, regardless of expense, in 'rooms' at Eastbourne). Away on the left, two prim little girls, apparently only dimly aware that something unfortunate is up, are quietly making card houses, a placid and well-behaved example to all. Seated at the table is to be seen an ashen-faced husband clutching, crumpled in his hand, a letter and plainly one not intended for him but for his wife. All is, in fact, discovered.

No problem here save the actual identity of her beau. Saucy milkmen with five minutes to spare had not yet come into their own as handy domestic safety-valve releasers. The family solicitor, then? A whiskery neighbour? A hot-blooded curate inflamed with communion wine filched from the vestry? No good asking the lady as she, hands convulsively clasped

*Inflamed by the communion wine*

35

together in despair, has done the wise thing and has fainted. There she lies, flat out on the floor and with not a spark left in her. Did the letter say, as they so often did in fiction, 'Fly with me!' It would at that time have been merely a figure of speech, the pair eloping by second class train and smuttily trans-Continental to a *pensione* in one of the cheaper parts of the Italian Riviera.

As might be expected, such pictures often made moral uplift their aim, Holman Hunt providing, in 'The Awakening Conscience', a thoughtful moment, coupled with a feast for the eyes, far from easy though it is to work out exactly what is afoot. A lady (early twenties) has been perched on a gentleman's knee while he, with what must have been some difficulty, played the upright piano, possibly rather a flashy Chopin *étude*, twiddly bits galore. I tend though to think that the music was probably something of a more religious nature, Ketelby's haunting 'In a Monastery Garden' maybe, for the lady, a divine light in her eye, has risen from her unconventional piano-stool and is moving away. What are we to think? Is she a kept woman? Are we in a love-nest and situated, at a guess from the meagre visual evidence available, in the Battersea area? Or have I mistaken the divine light and the lady is merely wondering about the nasty smells coming from the kitchen ('Heavens, Jasper, I never turned the oven down.')? The gig-lamped gentleman has a rather rakish look and appears to have his right foot permanently down on the loud pedal, such an indication of unreliable character that I fear we must infer the worst.

# Oh *what a beautiful evening*

To be invited to attend, by some kind person involved in the production, a London theatrical first night is almost invariably a hazardous experience. Behind one's polite and smiling face and beneath the trim dinner-jacket lies the thudding heart. One longs for friends to do well and is as anxious as they. I say 'almost' because every now and then an offering comes along that is financially and artistically fail-proof. *My Fair Lady* was one such. It had already run two years in New York. Errand-boys, if they had still existed, could have whistled its tunes from their bicycles. The dresses and décor were by our very own brilliant Beaton. The English stars were known and much loved, had created the original roles and success was written all over them. There had been eight faultless previews. The theatre was already sold out for over a year. The Drury Lane curtain, when it rose on that glamorous first night, need not, in a sense, ever have risen at all.

A first night that I, and doubtless its performers, would rather forget was Orton's *What the Butler Saw*. The upper parts of the house bore all in silence until the final fifteen minutes and then exploded into rage. I noted an interesting bodily manifestation. When the displeased noises loudly started, the imperturbable cast merely quickened its pace a little but the tips of the ears of Coral Browne and Sir Ralph (both quite unaccustomed to being rudely shouted at) turned an extraordinary bright salmon pink, fully visible from where I sat, shrinking, half way back in the dress circle. Sometimes the audience's objections are kept till actual curtain-fall. No star however great, is safe from the gallery's comments. Gladys Cooper herself, given to mumbling a little when a play wasn't up to much, did not always escape ('We love you, Gladys, but you *must* speak up'). Sometimes the objections are comical.

There was once a longish play, written for two characters only, a husband and wife. The scene was their living room, the plot their everyday lives. Nothing much happened and the audience was inclined to doze off a little, but suddenly in the third act there was a sharp ring at the front door bell. 'Whoever can that be?' said the wife, upon which a pleading and desperate voice from above shouted 'Let them in, whoever they are'.

It was the humble view of Rodgers and Hammerstein and of many others who have lived their lives in the theatre that 'the audience is always right'. If, for whatever reason, the customers are unhappy, the blame must never be laid at their door. The blood of theatre-lovers will run cold when they learn, from Frederick Nolan's fascinating *The Sound of Their Music* (Dent, £6.50), how close *Oklahoma* came to never happening at all and, many years previously, Richard Rodgers' career with it (but for a chance telephone call, he would long ago have abandoned his attempts at composing and gone into the profitable and only slightly less noisy world of babies' underwear). Indeed, fortunate chances favoured this revolutionary musical everywhere. Poor Larry Hart, a dedicated dipsomaniac and a deviant frequenter of what our author politely calls 'manners-be-damned parties', with whom Rodgers had faithfully collaborated for twenty-five years, was physically and mentally finished and there, ready to replace him, was Oscar Hammerstein, his talents not much tested since *Show Boat*. There too was the Theatre Guild, owners of the ideal material on which to base an unmistakably American musical, a play called *Green Grow the Lilacs*, though the Theatre Guild were less successful with their suggestion of two stars for leading roles (Shirley Temple and Groucho Marx). And then there was the happy fact that Rodgers preferred to put tunes to lyrics already written (with Hart it had had to be the other way round), and Hammerstein preferred this method too. Incredible to find that it took him a full week to decide ('Oh what a beautiful morning') that it was permissible to start the first two lines of the play ('Oh what a beautiful day') with the word 'Oh'. More incredible still was the fact that Rodgers completed the melody in exactly ten minutes ('It took nothing to write . . . The results are better if it comes in a rush'). Asked later how long it had taken him to compose the whole of *Oklahoma*, with its dozen or so numbers, the ballet music and overture, Richard Rodgers said that, with the best will in the world, he couldn't possibly make the time spent on composition come to a second longer than five hours.

*Oklahoma* was originally called *Away We Go!* As it turned its back on the European operetta and the gaudily convention-al escapist pieces that American audiences were accustomed to and which, in films, dear Jeanette MacDonald, all flashing teeth and bright bird-song, brought so winningly to an expec-tant world, backers for the venture were hard to find. 'The only risky thing in the theatre is not to take risks' and the curtain was to rise on an empty stage, apart from a staunch aunt churning at a churn. No rows of inanely smiling chorus girls were to be seen, and in due course there would be both a villain and a murder. Mike Todd summed up the general feeling with 'No girls, no gags, no good'. Even the warm-hearted Jerome Kern described the score as 'condescending'. And it was pointed out that there were already over 100 songs called 'Oklahoma'. Eventually the money was raised and the reluc-tant backers became, quite rapidly, millionaires. During the tryout at Boston, the entire cast caught German measles, their spots concealed by extra heavy make-up, but Boston took them to its welcoming heart and became for ever the pre-Broadway home of Rodgers and Hammerstein shows ('I wouldn't open anything, not even a can of tomatoes, anywhere but in Boston'). The play then moved to New York and the rest we know.

I was fortunate enough, hopelessly stage-struck as I have been since the age of four (*Peter Pan* at the King's Theatre, Hammersmith), to be invited to the London first night, again at Drury Lane, on April 30th, 1947. Here was another fail-proof. The songs and lyrics were widely known. Excited travellers back from New York spoke incoherently of its charm and magic. It was said, rightly, that it did not matter that it contained no established stars. The lights lowered and they took the curtain up on that virtually empty stage, ablaze with sunshine and ripening corn, and the cowboy, Curly, came strolling on to tell us what a beautiful morning it was. It was the first really agreeable thing to happen in London since the end of the war, an extraordinary uprush of happiness, and when the curtain finally fell, the cheers and applause combined in a weird and deafening wall of sound such as I have never heard before or since. Nor have I ever again seen seasoned critics actually weeping for joy. Nice to know they can.

But what, you ask, of *Carousel*? What of *South Pacific* and *The King and I*? What, above all, of *The Sound of Music*? Long ago at the Winter Garden Theatre there was a jolly musical called *Tell Me More*. The hero and heroine sang the title song, and it went:

He: 'You're the girl I adore'
She: 'Tell me more'
He: 'Other girls I deplore'
She: 'Tell me more'.

This powerful lyric ended with 'And though you've told me all you know, tell me more, tell me more, tell me more.' In a week or so, I hope to do just that.

# Scribble scribble

In the past I have been, and to my own sad cost and deprivation, far too trusting over the friendly lending both of books and of gramophone records. They tend to disappear. Copies of the books are usually, after endless time and expense and ferreting about, recoverable from other and second-hand sources. Not so with most of the gramophone records that are missing and here I am of course referring to the best type of all, the dear old 78s that daily ring out so melodiously in the spacious living-rooms of 'Myrtlebank'. Here the range of second-hand availabilities is very limited indeed and it would be a waste of my time to try to run to earth a long since vanished treasure, a pleasing music-hall song (can it have been sung by the splendid Randolph Sutton?) whose verse began with the striking words 'I'm coming o'er the ocean, a little girl to see. There'll be a great commotion, for her to marry me'. The first line of the tremendously jolly chorus went 'Mary, sweet and fascinating little fairy'. This is just the kind of lyric I like best, with delightful rhymes and the story-line perfectly clear – a love-sick swain explains that he is arriving by sea (he apologises later for his tardiness) to wed, in a rather showy manner, he hints, the blue-eyed (yes, they're mentioned too) girl of his choice. What could be poetically better?

To all of us there comes a moment in life when it is time to cast aside the mask and reveal oneself, naked and ashamed, for what one is and I have to tell you, with enormous regret (for the loss is mine), that I don't really very much care for the plays of Shakespeare when performed in their entirety. Small isolated chunks of the Bard are fine, but not large chunks amalgamated into a three hour whole. His knowledge of human nature takes one's breath away but one can't be breathless for three hours at a stretch without seriously undermining health. And there are other disadvantages. I get very fidgety after the eighth 'By my troth,' and 'go to, go to,' and 'Marry, come up, I trow.' I think that the subject was damaged for me by not very enthusiastic teaching at school. The copies of the plays that were doled out to us were always abridged editions, and one hoped that this meant that quite a bit of the text had been removed, but it merely indicated that some latter-day professorial Bowdler had snipped out all the nasty bits (Ophelia's saucy song, for example) and left us free to press purely on. It was the same thing in frog. When we did the *contes choisis* of Maupassant, it was from an *édition pour la jeunesse* and a puritanical hand had *choisi* only the relatively innocent stories. We didn't get to *Boule de Suif* until later in life and under our own steam and when, presumably, dirt didn't matter so much.

I am all for the plays of Shakespeare being very thoroughly abridged, if not actually altered. I have several suggestions to make. Take *Macbeth*, for instance. Let us have, by all means, the first four scenes as they are, but what about a nice variation when we arrive at Inverness in Act I Scene V and Lady Macbeth enters reading the letter from Macbeth that brings out her very worst side? Instead, why not let her be 'discovered', an early victim of postal delays, at the front door and cross-questioning that extremely tiresome old hall porter about the postman. Has he come? 'He hath come and gone, good madam', the porter replies. 'Wast there then naught for me?' asks Lady Macbeth, looking wistful. 'Naught, sweet lady', he answers, which she swiftly counters with 'Tis a naughty naught.' The porter then attempts to cheer her up with one of those fearfully complicated and unfunny Shakespearean smutty jokes. 'Methinks a postman be like an inconsiderate and hasty lover who visiteth his mistress in her bedchamber and findeth her in riggish and unbuttoned mood.' Lady Macbeth, anxious to give the thing a kick, asks 'How so, varlet?' 'Why, marry, he too doth unbutton and, like this our postman, comes, and then goes too'. Lady Macbeth, never short of a quip, screeches, 'Go to yourself, knave' and the pair of them then collapse into those wild and maniacal shrieks of laughter that play directors find convenient for deadening, so to speak, the deafening silence in the audience. Then Lady Macbeth wanders off to the kitchen to supervise her breakfast and prod the baps and, her mind on domestic matters, all that little bother with Duncan is avoided.

*King Lear* would greatly benefit from quite an elaborate shortening and this is easily achieved as early as Act I Scene I when the poor old boy, not yet completely cracked, shuffles in to the 'Room of State', takes a pew and, after some preliminaries, says 'Know that we have divided in three our kingdom.' How very much better if he mooched about a bit, took a long hard look at Goneril and Regan (two obviously odious girls, both smirking away like anything and with 'troublemaker' written all over them) and then plonked himself down and said 'Know that we have decided not to divide in three our kingdom.' After which he kisses Cordelia and we can all get up and go home. *The Merchant of Venice* presents no problems at all. The caskets provide excellent abridgement possibilities. In Act II the dusky Prince of Morocco, no fool, promptly chooses the leaden casket and instantly whisks a delighted Portia, thrilled to be a Princess, away from dreary old Belmont to a life of luxurious ease in Marrakesh, with asses' milk baths, whole roast sheep for dinner, and banana custard simply *ad lib*.

Is not Shakespeare, you ask, turning in his grave? I much doubt it. Far too sensible a man to mind, surely. And anyhow, and strange though it may seem, such cavalier and impertinent treatment of their work was just what authors, to a rather less exaggerated degree than I have been guilty of, had to put up with until well into this century. Their difficulties and complaints, their inability to band themselves militantly together against such practices as piracy, illegal editions and adaptations, and their feeble and dilatory rallying to the copyright cause are the subject of Victor Bonham-Carter's excellent book *Authors By Profession* (The Society of Authors, £5.95), a splendid survey of this most chancy way of earning a living and which ranges from the introduction of printing to the Copyright Act of 1911.

'Writing is *par excellence*', Mr Bonham-Carter correctly judges, 'our national art' (30,000 titles are published annually in Britain alone, to the great confusion, not to say dismay, of literary editors) and fairly scurvily have writers been treated down the years. *Paradise Lost* earned its author the princely sum of £18. Jane Austen, unable to place her first book, which was called *Pride and Prejudice*, sold *Northanger Abbey* for £10 to a Bath publisher, who then got cold feet and demanded the £10 back. In Grubb Street, which positively existed, and near Moorfields, hacks scratched away in garrets at starvation rates and slept three to a bed. Swift, Fielding and Trollope could only live by being gainfully occupied in other capacities. Keats, as we know, was a hospital dresser and Wordsworth held the unusual post of 'distributor of stamps for the county of Westmorland'. As Isaac d'Israeli, who, in addition to fathering the statesman, moved in literary circles, wrote in his *Calamities of Authors*, 'Authors continue poor, and Book-sellers become opulent; an extraordinary result.' There would be some who claim that the position is not so very different today.

Success has, on the other hand, brought rewards sometimes somewhat in excess of what is justified. Tennyson refused an offer of £20,000 for a lecture tour in the USA, and why bother when he could get £700 for a single poem in the magazine *Good Words*, and £1,000 for a three-stanza one from the lectureless USA? Another high earner was Henry James. How delightful to find him, in 1888, taking 20 pages in which to decline a dinner invitation in honour of American authors, coupled with a vehement attempt to dissuade the kind hosts from having a dinner at all.

# Willingly to school

As a child, my mother, considered by her doting mid-Victorian parents to be far too precious to be risked in a rough boarding-school, was instead exposed in 'the schoolroom' at home to a succession of loveless and needy governesses (in 1850 there were 40,000 of them in circulation) who, for £20 a year, taught her all they knew, before packing up those depressing wickerwork trunks and glooming off elsewhere. 'All they knew' seemed to consist of the capes and bays of Scotland, which had to be learnt parrot-fashion, and Canada's exports and imports, ditto. My mother was by nature cheerful and out-going and longed for wider spheres but a request to be allowed to attend a local day school was received with horror and turned instantly down, my grandmother doubtless sniffing smelling salts to help her to recover from the shock. Even when, greatly daring, my mother was occasionally able to get permission to play afternoon tennis at a friend's house, she was for days merrily referred to as 'Miss Gadabout'.

This educational non-event was the lot of many girls in reasonably affluent families, and indeed the alternative did have a certain element of risk in it. These were the popular Ladies' Academies, a sort of juvenile finishing school of which in 1836 there were over a hundred on the Sussex coast alone. Though some of them cost more than Eton, they had in general spartan living conditions, poor food and lax discipline. Here the girls, moulded into an acceptable shape by steel corsets and held in place by various braces and clamps and contraptions to aid deportment, were taught 'the accomplishments'. They sewed. They painted. They thumped the piano, scraped the fiddle and twanged the harp. Kilted buffers taught them Scottish reels, and pomaded frogs the gavotte. Sleek Spaniards, breathing heavily, told them how to handle castanets, and who can say what else. Army sergeants even instructed them in 'marching', a method of forward motion to which the female form is totally unsuited (how conscientiously they marched, this way and that, in the war, and how fearfully ludicrous they looked, especially sideways on). And then suddenly, at fashionable Cheltenham, at modish, raffish Brighton and elsewhere, all was changed. Proper boarding-schools for girls, with high educational aims, sprang into exciting life and, with them and as though by a miracle, the Great Headmistresses that such places require.

I have written before of having, in the 1930s, visited various girls' schools, for literary purposes, and having come up against the alarming and commanding and relentless and unflappable figures who ran them. Here, and once more we are in debt to the superb delvings and researches of Jonathan Gathorne-Hardy reported in his *The Public School Phenomenon*, are some of their predecessors. There was Lydia Rous of the Mount School, a Quaker establishment of distinction, who terrified her staff to such an extent that an American visitor thought they must all be under some Trappist vow of silence. There was the tyrannical Kate Unwin of Walthamstow Hall who, coming upon a group of young teachers planning to have a cosy read of *Jane Eyre*, forbade them to look at it again until they were older (twenty-five). And then there was the famous Miss Lawrence whose family, in sore need of cash, started Roedean (motto: 'Honour Roedean'), a scholastic experience which was meted out to some of my married friends and of which they now speak with assorted emotions. 'In Brighton, all schools succeed,' Miss Lawrence's aunt announced on the school's move there from Wimbledon in 1889. How right she was. It proved, expensive from the start (£126 a year), a goldmine. Rapidly increasing numbers (how splendidly the Victorians *bred*) forced a move along the coast towards Rottingdean and many acres of land were purchased, upon which the girls, as firmly disciplined and regimented as any in history's pages, struggled at hockey and cricket (one of the book's many delightful snaps shows an Eton-cropped wicket-keeper deftly at work behind the stumps, the last word in skilful dexterity). Miss Lawrence herself, painted by Orpen, looks like a masculine Queen Victoria. She had an extremely loud voice (the better to tick you off with, my dear), was president of the Lacrosse Association, weighed latterly 18 stone and always expected people to, of all things, admire her hats. Who dare say that Angela Brazil in any way exaggerated?

Above all, there was the formidable, dauntless Miss Beale (she learned to bicycle at 62) of 'Cheltenham College for Young Ladies', a stone building easily mistaken for a fortress and which allows not the merest peep in (or out) and which was founded in 1854. Miss Beale soon added on a kindergarten and a teacher training college, winding up in command of 900 girls. And up, like mushrooms, popped in due course other institutions – Wycombe Abbey, St. Paul's, Sherborne, Westonbirt. Miss Beale, who as a child dreamt of nothing but running schools, was a dedicated fanatic. She used sometimes, to the confusion of her visitors, speak of Cheltenham as 'my husband'. It was no more than the truth, even if it caused anxious looks. Her influence lives on. Even today, 800 girls change classes in an awesome silence, swishing soundlessly up and down the passages as though Miss Beale herself were watching. In the 1950s there was, in mid-winter, a parade of girls before the headmistress. Girl after girl had, in turn, to raise her skirt and reveal that she was wearing the regulation green

*Girl after girl had, in turn, to raise her skirt*

knickers, about which there had been some slackness. One can see Miss Beale nodding approval. What did it matter that it was customary for some of the girls to give each other masculine nick-names (Jacko, Bob, Charlie)? One girl even referred to the others as 'chaps'. Awkward emotions like these were soon swept away in the tidal-wave of work that engulfed the school.

Girls conform on the whole more readily than boys. History reveals few female rebellions and so how doubly shocking was a *Times* item of news in the summer which stated that 40 girls at a boarding school had been sent home a week early (hardly a punishment, one would have thought) for throwing the gym mistress into the swimming pool. Shades of dear Miss Brazil again.

# By Jupiter

Alerted at dawn by sharp military rappings on my door, I spent the morning of my 30th birthday on May 10, 1940, in Lille in N.E. France preparing for the fray and by the evening I was in Belgium. A thirtieth birthday seemed at the time to be one of the more traumatic of life's milestones and Hitler, who plainly knew that it was my birthday and was determined at all costs to be irritating, chose that very day for invading the Low Countries and so various festivities most kindly arranged for me which were to centre round luscious French food and rich wines had to be abandoned. *C'était la guerre.* I do not now recall what my horoscope for the day announced but it was probably, as is the way with most horoscopes, something both informative and comforting: 'A quiet day for taking stock of yourself. Romance may be hovering in the offing, so strive to control the moodiness that has been bothering you lately. Keep your social life flexible. If you have green fingers, today, with the risk of frost almost gone, is ideal for planting out those geraniums. Lightly fork over your tilth, mulch thoroughly and get going!' The streets of Lille were full, not of tilth but of agitated Frogs filling up their Citroëns with petrol, strapping mattresses to the roofs and manifestly dead nuts on getting going in any direction that wasn't east. German aeroplanes had already been over to take a peck at what was afoot below and a leaden despair was in the air. Plucky little Napoleon wouldn't have known which way to look.

During the war that followed, London and the blitz were greatly enlivened by those marvellous Alan Melville revues at the Ambassadors Theatre featuring Hermione Gingold. In one of these, she appeared, with a friend, as an old and somewhat slatternly evacuee lady perched on a country seat and messily munching sandwiches extracted from her gas-mask case. Asked by the friend when her birthday was, she gave the date and was then told 'Ah, that makes you a Virgo.' To which Miss Gingold replied, in those rich brown and sepulchral tones that sound as though her vocal cords had for years been marinated in Guinness, 'Does it? That's clever of it!' Nowadays we are all apt to know already whether we are a Leo or a Pisces and are familiar with the technical lingo that accompanies our various birthday predictions and which often appears to be so very unseemly: 'Mercury and Jupiter conjunct in Uranus, while Gemini is lodged in Venus, planet of love and your solar twelfth house. Tread warily today. You will visit acquaintances and have fun in a friendly and informal way'. Oh dear. Informal fun, I fear, and as far as my Devon life is concerned can only mean ping-pong in the Bultitudes' rumpus room, with pot luck to follow, Giles doing the honours ('Another banger anybody?') in a funny apron with jokes to match.

I rather regret the disappearance of the Victorian birthday books popular well into this century and in which friends' birthday dates were carefully written down for future action. Each day contained some quotation, chosen apparently totally at random and frequently of a tremendously depressing nature. Turning excitedly to May 10, I am at once slapped down with 'The gates of hell are open night and day' or 'Change and decay in all around I see'. Or it might be the cheery Rossetti poem 'Does the road wind up-hill all the way? Yes, to the very end.' In some birthday books, it wasn't merry passages so much as Interesting Facts of the 'Typhoon in Fiji' kind. Here again May 10 is a bit of a sell (Outbreak of Indian Mutiny).

Birthdays and the presents and festivities that accompany them take different people different ways. To Linda Rannells Lewis and her book, appropriately called *Birthdays* (Routledge and Kegan Paul, £5.75), I owe the information that at Presbyterian Sunday Schools in West Virginia, any child so ill-advised as to have a birthday had to stand up, stiff with embarrassment, and say:

> I must be good and glad and gay
> For I'm a birthday child today.

Queen Victoria, ever one to set the pace and once at a bit of a loss as to what to give one of her granddaughters to mark the occasion of the girl's sixteenth birthday, hit on the ideal present and parcelled up and sent off a bust of her dead mother and a collection of illustrations of funerals that she had attended, just the thing to set a teenager's pulses racing. On the other hand, the Queen herself was far from pleased to receive from her eldest son nothing but a rather ordinary table from Ireland, scene of the first of what was to be a sensational series of sexual misdemeanours ('Oh! Bertie alas! alas!'). Poor old Job wasn't, for obvious reasons, too keen on birthdays ('Why died I not in the womb?', or something), but little Lord Fauntleroy on the contrary was delighted to see throngs of tenants turning up and flags flying from the castle turrets. 'Is it because they like me, Dearest?' the little beast wistfully asked his mother, a woman much too lacking in maternal solicitude to give him a stinging blow in the face.

I recently gave at 'Myrtlebank' a small tea-party – icy cold and drenching rain and the fire had to be lit. While the tea (Earl Grey or Typhoo) and the viands (cucumber sandwiches, a heaped plateful of rather battered garibaldis and two kinds of cake) were circulating both without and within, I thought it might be agreeable to divert the guests by telling them with whom they shared birthdays. For example, Miss Entwhistle, born on February 3, shared it with Gertrude Stein, Mendelssohn and Hughie Green. It was also the day in which John of Gaunt died but none of this information seemed to give her any pleasure. Indeed, she looked extremely startled. And so it was with some of the others. Canon Mountjoy (April 20), finding himself linked up thereby with Mohammed, Harold Lloyd and Hitler, retired smartly into his shell and muttered what can only have been a hasty string of prayers. Mrs Mountjoy (May 26) fared a little better with The Venerable Bede, Queen Mary and Al Jolson, though Al Jolson had to be explained to her. My Cousin Madge (April 29), was, as usual, triumphant with Wellington, Duke Ellington, Jeremy Thorpe, Beecham and Emperor Hirohito. But then back we went into gloom by finding that Bunty Bultitude (Giles was either out on the links or killing something: I forget which) was teamed up with James Joyce, Nell Gwynne and Havelock Ellis, all of which, apart from Miss Gwynne, had to be explained to Mrs Mountjoy.

There are some very jolly birthday trios about. Take March 20 – Michael Redgrave, Ovid and Vera Lynn. What could be cosier? Or August 4, – Shelley, Harry Lauder and the Queen Mother. On September 7 we find Elizabeth I, Edith Sitwell and

Grandma Moses. One of the most bizarre couplings occurs on February 6 (Marlowe, Queen Anne and Freddy Trueman), only rivalled by April 2 (Charlemagne, Casanova and Alec Guinness). Let astrologers, or whatever, make of those what they can.

There is, however, one birthday trio that silences all opposition and is so much above all others in interest and brilliance that the rest of us (I am matched with Fred Astaire and Thomas Lipton) must hang our heads. It is December 16. Just the three names. Beethoven, Noël Coward and Jane Austen. Beat that if you can!

# Be fruitful and multiply

Until I was about thirty-five, which, for the inquisitive, was three decades and a bit ago, I didn't really much care for wine. I have since made up for it in quite a big and elaborate way but in those days I would have gladly settled for a glass of orangeade instead. I disliked, for one thing, the time-consuming pantomime that often went with the production of some cobwebby bottle lying sideways in its wickerwork nest. There then came the examination of the cork and the consultation of those little cards that the cognoscenti used to carry about with them and which informed them whether 1932 was a 'good' year for claret or whatever and then presumed, on whose authority I do not know, to allot marks for this brand of wine or that. And after that one endured the repellent sniffings and the unlovely snufflings, the rolling round the tongue, the holding of the glass up to the light, all of them actions performed to the accompaniment of a flood of pretentious jabber about which Maurice Bowra, that forceful realist and non-admirer of affectations, had a word to say (I'm bored by all that wine rubbish. There's only one thing in wine that I'm interested in now. *Quantity*.').

We don't have many grapes in Appleton but regular readers who may have been worrying, in their kind and courteous way, about what sort of a fruit crop we have been gathering from our richly soiled (and I speak agriculturally rather than in terms of something needing Daz) south west, need worry no more. Unfurrow the brow. Our crop has been, frankly, totally tip-top and the fruits of the earth have, in their due season, been our happy portion on a friendly give and take and share and share alike basis. Throughout the summer we have been nourished at frequent intervals by the Bultitudes' nectarines and peaches, nurtured beneath glass I need hardly say and perched on tissue paper before being graciously distributed in

*One endured the repellent sniffings*

generously-sized chip-baskets with a merry little note tucked inside ('Happy nibblings! Giles and Bunty'). The soft fruit season gives my Cousin Madge a chance to shine, her straw-bugs and her liberal gifts of them being rightly famous all along the valley. Her strawberries are, I think, Royal Sovereign but I wonder if a variety still exists that used to call itself Madame Kooi, such a charming name and whom one saw either as a petite little Japanese lady, parasol open and quietly tending her berries in the intervals of wondering what on earth can be keeping Lieutenant Pinkerton, or as an Australian housewife down by the billabong, short of a husband and screaming 'Cooey'.

Well then, my neighbours at *Dun Roamin* are noted for their Conference pears, an offering of which will be along any minute now (such a poor arrangement on the part of Dame Nature that the best pears have only a brief 48 hours when they may be said to be at perfect concert pitch), and dear Miss Entwhistle is here, there and everywhere with her plums, her blue Czars early on, and then later the bulging and opulent perfection of her Victorias, each one a juicy *bonne bouche* of health-giving Vitamin C. A tiny way down the scale of excellence, even though each one is blessed by the church, come Canon Mountjoy's damsons from his relentlessly prolific trees, each damson about the size and hardness of those round metallic pellets that used to be fed, and perhaps still are, into siphons for making soda-water in the home. Ideal for a solid, all-purpose jam, of course, and all right for stewing if you're really up against it for a pudding, but I do sometimes rather wonder whether that Dutch disease (so impertinent of it not to keep itself to itself in Holland) might not be persuaded, instead of finally finishing off all our beautiful elms, to switch to damsons.

But where, you rightly ask, does 'Myrtlebank' stand in all this display of generosity? Where is that give and take of which I spoke? What is there to set against those nectarines, peaches, strawberries, pears, plums and, er, damsons? I have no need to hang my head in shame and my answer is a simple one. Apples. For these my friends look to me and they seldom look in vain. I am fortunate to have an orchard which, relatively protected from frost, covers three acres in the very heart of Appleton and, intersected by a stream, slopes gently upwards from the flower-filled grounds of 'Myrtlebank'. It provides a feast of blossom for the eye in April and early May, and now there is a feast of another kind, every bough laden beneath as bumper a harvest as we have ever before experienced. I am now trying, in imitation of the French *vendange* and its grape-gathering, to popularise, when it comes to apple-gathering, the word *pommange*. 'We can't come to lunch, Sylvia, because of the *pommange*' would sound rather well down the telephone wires. It is, as you see, a skilful blending of the words *pomme* and *manger* and it would give the whole undertaking a distinctive frog cachet.

Rich red ripeness is everywhere. 'Stay me with flagons, comfort me with apples' sings *The Song of Solomon*, and if the writer, who must by now be a senior citizen and can therefore take advantage of BR's concessionary rates for the elderly, cares to board the 10.30 from Paddington and then make a bee-line for us, we can do just that. The early and brightly-hued Beauty of Bath, first in the field and such a source of pleasure to wasps, were of course picked in August, but fully available are the succulence of James Grieve and the mouth-watering Ellison's Orange, not to speak of the Bramleys and Monarchs that, sliced and sugared, nestle so nutritiously beneath the pudding's pie-crust. Picking all these delights presents several problems. Apples, like actresses, bruise easily and should not be allowed to thud to the ground. It is, however, impossible to pick without dislodging occasionally some shy pippin coyly concealing itself behind a twig and I know of few things in life more immediately painful than receiving a sizeable Lane's Prince Albert, descending from a height of fifteen feet, on the bridge of the nose. The apples that fall most readily and unerringly onto one's head are called, and what could be more suitable, Newton Wonder. The laws of gravity don't seem to have changed one little bit. Oh and by the way, our cider apples, all four tons of them, are this year to be despatched to admirable Whiteway's; so if next year you notice an attractive new zest and freshness in their product, kindly spare a grateful thought for 'Myrtlebank'.

# Alive, alive, oh

Few of the great theatre beauties of the recent past – among them, Gladys Cooper, Vivien Leigh and Diana Wynyard – were at all vain about their stunning looks and, going back a bit further, Stella Patrick Campbell, a sensational sight in her day, was even able to make jokes ('I look like a burst paper bag') about her spreading figure and vanished charms. She made up for it in a way by developing the sharpest tongue in Shaftesbury Avenue and on Broadway and she became a dreaded visitor to dressing-rooms, gleeful in disaster and especially on first nights when the gallery had been both disapproving and noisy ('I *say*, didn't they boo!' was her jovial greeting to Miss Laurette Taylor, a visiting American star). On another occasion and on being introduced to a famous actress whom she had never met, Mrs Campbell muttered and in a booming voice that was accustomed to reaching the furthest corners of vast theatres, 'Thought she was dead.'

No, not dead, and not even ailing. But as to the genuine defunct, Hamlet once remarked when, as so often, in pensive mood (did he, one wonders, ever ask himself whether his legs were fully suited to those black tights? I've seen some very rum underpinnings in my time, including those of Sir Frank Benson, a collector's item) that there is a noticeable and regrettable lack of persons who manage to return from Beyond and spill the beans about the hereafter, though on this subject I did once get a short, sharp shock. I had been saddened during the war by the supposedly correct news that reached me in the army of the sudden death in Oundle of the delightful man who ran a gramophone and record shop and who had kindly supplied me down the years with countless celluloid Hits from the Shows, many of which are with me still (Elsie Randolph in *That's A Good Girl* is especially tuneful) and, though some of them are over fifty years old, sound as good as nearly new. In those happy days, if you ordered a record on Monday, you got it on Wednesday. If you did that nowadays, improved transport conditions, the devoted work force and progress generally would ensure that you waited three weeks for it, and then possibly received the wrong record, badly bent.

Returning to Oundle after the war and making my sedate way by three-speed bicycle down one of its two main thoroughfares (it's as beautiful a small stone town as you could wish to find), whom should I suddenly see upon the pavement but my gramophone friend, not in the least dead but bright as a button and doubtless on his way to deliver some Hits from the Shows, by now *Oklahoma* and *Brigadoon*, to an expectant customer. To find him alive and kicking was a heart-stopping moment. I briskly dismounted, we had a warm reunion and I then found myself asking 'Are you better?' He looked, as well he might, nonplussed, not realising that as far as I was concerned he was fresh back from the undiscovered country from whose bourn no traveller returns, and so on, and where I rather doubt whether they have gramophones and 10 inch records of the Astaires singing numbers from *Lady Be Good*, with George Gershwin at the piano. And more's the pity.

And bless me if, the other night, a similar sort of ghostlike shock didn't take my breath away all over again. Dinner (home-made leek-and-potato soup, shoulder of lamb and the necessary additions, onion sauce being a must, and then *les fromages*) in 'Myrtlebank' was over, the last glass of a reputable claret had gone down the red lane (well, it's my only proper meal of the day), and a sense of repletion and well-being was mine. Then, like many another fan up and down the country, I moved to the television set and switched on for *Dallas*. There they all were and in glorious colour – Miss Ellie (such a relief that she seems to have kicked the drink habit that briefly threatened her), Lucy (shacked up now in marital bliss and in that condominium), J. R. (the devil himself in human form) and poor old Sue Ellen, blubbing as usual though I've taken to wondering whether by now, so determined and unbridled has been her boozing, it isn't tears of gin that pour in wet profusion down her face.

It will be recalled by devotees, and will surely come as a happy surprise to those few who know not *Dallas* and who may thus be coaxed into viewing this enthralling series, that at one point poor old Sue Ellen, reacting strongly to the discovery of yet another of J. R.'s infidelities (girl secretaries, shorthand pads at the ready, disturb him quite terribly), tottered tipsily into a bar largely frequented by cowboys and secured for herself an, er, admirer called Dusty, who turned out not to be actually a cowboy himself but active in the cattle trade and tremendously rich, which is always such a comfort, don't you think? This wealth proved to Sue Ellen that Dusty admired her for herself alone and not because of her extremely close connection with Ewing Oil. So for quite a time she dried her tears and smiled and dimpled up no end at Dusty, and Dusty kept proving over and over again in his expensive apartment how much he admired Sue Ellen. But affluent cattle barons tend to own private aeroplanes, and private aeroplanes are never quite as safe as public ones, and one distressing and disastrous day, Dusty crashes and, according to a newspaper report, becomes dead and therefore unable any more to admire Sue Ellen in the way that they both found so stimulating and agreeable. So back she hurries, and who wouldn't, to the gin bottle.

Momentarily abandoning *Dallas* in order to stoke up the fire with logs fetched from the hall (the extensive grounds of 'Myrtlebank' supply all our needs in the way of wood, trees dying from time to time just like anybody else), I resumed my seat and adjusted my viewing spectacles, only to jump out of my chair with a cry of astonishment for there, large as life, was Dusty, returned from the dead. Well, not perhaps quite as large as life but paralysed and in a wheelchair and very busy explaining to Sue Ellen, every inch of her a sodden mass of tears and her face working convulsively, that the little mishap had made any further admiration out of the question. She might not think that this mattered, but it would. However much she might admire him still, he would never be able to admire her right back. This feeling of inadequacy in the field of admiration was, I can only think, the reason why he never sent her, at the very least, a newsy post-card from his hospital bed.

Meanwhile, back at the ranch . . .

# Smile please

In the days before gifted Cecil Beaton revolutionised portrait photography by snapping sitters, though sitting was the last thing that they were required to do, upside down and in a sea of balloons, photographs tended to be deadly serious and head-on, as in the less acceptable kind of motor accident. Many of our British photographers moved in what were relatively exalted circles and various revered names are stored away on memory's tablets – Foulsham & Banfield, Bassano, the Downeys (W and D), Bertram Park, Sasha and particularly Elliott & Fry who specialised in rather grim-looking major-generals, politicians and the more august and successful type of Bishop. Not for these experts the multitudinous shutter clicks of today and the profligate waste of film. Bishops were exposed, if you follow me, at the most six times in a sitting ('And now a little smile, my Lord?') and the choice for the frontispiece to that book of memoirs, 'From My Palace Window', was therefore a narrow one, a choice sometimes left to the Bishop's wife: 'I like Number 3 best, Ambrose. They've caught your twinkle.'

Which brings me to a long overdue apology. The happy snap of self which normally graces, if I may venture to use such a verb, this page was inserted rather against my will. Better for me, I urged the NS authorities, to remain, visually at least, Something of a Mystery but I was overruled. Hence the chubby likeness, the carefree air, the gleaming gig-lamps. So sorry. However you'll want, I dare say, to know into whose talented lens I peered in order to obtain for you this unusual ocular treat. I hastened, as I always do when needing anything, into admirable Exeter and into the roomy photographic *salons* of the Navana Studios ('We Are Opposite The Museum') and hey-presto!

Until a visit that I made quite recently, all my motor trips into Exeter have been a joy and delight. Bowling along the Teign valley, one runs over in the mind the different aims to be achieved – chicken joints from Sainsbury's, a tie or two (so *reasonable*) from Marks and Spencer, cash to be paid into the Abbey National, the latest Frederick Forsyth from the library, a refreshing bottle of Martini from Victoria Wine and then, if in really madcap mood, a currant bun and cup of coffee at those charming tea-rooms in The Close with a splendiferous view of the cathedral's cleaned and superb west front. But the other day, on crossing the city's boundary line, a sad shock presented itself. I have mentioned before the subject of Town Twinning, to me a pointless and quite idiotic linking with some remote frog place of which few have ever heard and for which nobody cares a fig. I have however grown accustomed to the announcement, after an ornamental board saying WELCOME TO EXETER, that we are twinned with Rennes, and so picture my dismay on finding, without warning or any public discussion that I know of, that we are now also twinned with BAD HOMBURG. German, and could anything be more unfortunate? To begin with, the actual choice of name is a disaster. Although you and I and other linguistic smartyboots know that *Bad* means bath or spa, the word 'bad' will to a number of people merely mean the opposite of good. And as for Homburg, we all know what that is – a species of felt hat worn by men, with a narrowish brim and a dent in the top, a depression ideal as a rain-water trap and a refreshment area for any passing birdies. So the full name will finally signify, to more than one, BAD HAT. I ask you!

And where, may I enquire, is all this going to end? If we are now prepared to twin with a country whose inhabitants were busy, a mere forty years ago, raining bombs down on Exeter, slaughtering hundreds and almost completely destroying it, what about other countries who have never got up to mischief? Portugal, for instance, 'our oldest ally'. Or plucky little Belgium. Luxembourg, perhaps, Sweden, possibly. One only hopes that somebody responsible will be in charge and that, as the twinning craze spreads, good sense and, above all, good taste will march hand in hand. Delightful though the place is, I am sure, one would oneself think twice about an urban link-up with Bumbum (Nigeria).

Pitfalls are to be found on every side. The current custom of broad-minded, not to say loose, talk with no holds barred has prepared almost everybody for almost everything but even then, who would give a cry of joy at finding themselves nominally joined to Orgaz (Spain) or Pronic, and where could that be but in frogland. Even the simple Hiko (USA) carries with it a rather damaging suggestion of insobriety. The Americans, bless them, are a good bit less sensitive about names than the rest of us and something tells me that, did we but know, oddities galore lurk in their hinterland – Pyorrhoea (Minnesota), Penis (Arizona) and Armpit (Michigan). Not that, with towns like Krapina (Yugoslavia) about, one needs to invent anything. And there are various Japanese place names beginning with the letter F that I really do not care to discuss here and on a page that is essentially, and will remain so, family reading.

How cheering it is to discover that not all in the twinning world is accepted with supine complacency. It seems that the mayor of that pleasing Hampshire town, Basingstoke, linked with Alençon for reasons unknown to most, has taken exception to remarks made and an opinion expressed about Ireland by his French opposite number, a M. Pierre Mauger, and has thereby imperilled what I can hardly think to have been a particularly secure or interesting or emotional union of, so far, thirteen years' duration. But what will happen, do you suppose, as the news of the rupture spreads down the Basingstoke streets? Will there be panic in the Co-op? Will prayers for a reconciliation be offered in the parish church? Will old ladies faint dead away in Boots (rather a good place to do it in)? I doubt it. There might be a feeling of relief. In mid-1940 it was no sort of hardship to realise that we were, at last, alone.

# Blow hot blow cold

I have, alas, to report a slight culinary mishap in the palatial kitchen, with its gleaming working surfaces, of 'Meadowlands', the imposing country residence of my Cousin Madge in our Devon village of Appleton. Wishful to prepare a trouble-free evening repast for herself and her household, she secured, on a lightning dash to the shop, one of those steak-and-kidney pies that come in a large round tin, the lid of which has to be removed with a tin-opener before it can safely be placed in the oven and the cooking process begin. At first sight the pie's pastry surface looks a little sullen and unresponsive but really hot heat transforms all and nothing but crusty succulence ensues. Suitable accompanying vegetables were prepared, together with a tasty gravy lavishly enriched with Bisto, after which the pie was lovingly laid on the oven's topmost shelf and at the heat recommended (400 degrees, or mark 6), the door was firmly closed and the 'Time-O' pinger gadget wound up and set to give its warning ping after the correct number of cooking minutes. My cousin, conscious of work well done, then settled herself down before the television-set in her sitting-room and became instantly absorbed, as which of us with taste and discrimination does not, in the splendid panorama of Life which calls itself 'Crossroads'. And not very long afterwards there was the sound of an extremely loud explosion.

Her first thought, keen viewer that she is, was that a major and very unexpected upheaval had occurred in the drama unfolding before her eyes at the Crossroads Motel (desperadoes holed up in Chalet 9 perhaps and now trying to shoot their way out) but then she realised that the noise had been a rather more local one and, pressing courageously into her kitchen, she found a scene of desolation as though her area had been suddenly visited by one of those natural American phenomena ('Hurricane Dulcie') with a misleadingly demure girl's name. The oven, with its door blown right off, was a tangled ruin and the pie, with who knows what desperate and last minute instinct of *sauve qui peut*, had hastily distributed itself all over the kitchen walls. Crockery had been shattered and littered the floor. And on a nearby table lay the tin-opener, unused and doubtless looking reproachful. Her thoughts elsewhere, my cousin had omitted to remove, despite the manufacturer's most clearly expressed and visible warnings, the pie's lid, and the relentless laws of physics had seen to the rest.

As it happens, I am no stranger, seasoned campaigner that I am, to such alarming occurrences. At the beginning of the war I was billeted in the Aldershot district with a very kind and agreeable family who, much as they must have resented military intrusion (I was masquerading as a Lieutenant) on their privacy, were polite enough to let no sign of it appear. They were, and it is the only word for it, dears. The family included an ancient male relative of the grandfatherly type who tended to retire early to bed and who liked to prepare his own supper ('a little eggy something on a tray') and take it upstairs with him. It was not always eggs, however.

He had one evening removed himself as usual and the rest of us were sitting about, sipping away at a heartening glass of best sherry-type and discussing why Hitler was not married ('A really good wife might have made *all* the difference'), when a deafening bang from the kitchen alerted us to the fact that grandpa had got himself into a bit of a muddle. In comparison with the many bangs that one was to hear later, this one could rank with the very best and on this occasion it was caused by a tin of baked beans that, recklessly unpierced and placed in boiling water, had exploded with grenade-like power and efficiency. The beans had, in this case, decided to hasten upwards and had spread themselves all over the ceiling, forming a pattern of great complexity and beauty and charm, as though a top-notch London decorator had been expensively at work ('Truly, my dear, you've never done anything finer'). As the beans were not yet a rationed comestible and therefore were, so to speak, expendable, the family's first anxious concern was, naturally, the cat. Deaf as a door-post, it had slept peacefully in its basket beneath the kitchen table throughout the entire affair. So *that* was all right. The bean-fancier too, who shared the cat's disability, had come through the ordeal

64

*but with an excess of cold*

with flying colours and was busily making do with sardines. We all felt that we had been blooded for the very worst that Hitler's bombs might subsequently try to achieve.

If the Devil has any sense at all, and there are no grounds whatever for thinking him in any way a fool, it is not with an excess of heat that his pitchforked staff and reception committee will greet us in the nether regions but with an excess of cold. Much nastier. I fancy, incidentally, that those of us who are clearly bound for down below (I have had a quite marvellous life and am extremely grateful but both my upbringing and the teaching of the Church lead me to think that I will undoubtedly have to pay for it in some way later on) are going to bump into a much more stimulating lot ('Why hello there, Attila!') than those destined for what one thinks of as the wing-and-halo section. Well, which would you prefer to face for an eternity of têtes-à-têtes, Nero or Grace Darling, Lady Macbeth or the Venerable Bede, Alfred the Great or Henry VIII, though I fear that these alternatives sound all too like those hectoring questions at O Level (State your reasons and draw a map).

And when it comes to the miseries of feeling really cold, I am quite sure that some older readers will agree with me that there are few chills in life to compare with a school dormitory in the depths of a winter term, filled with cheerless rows of uniformly coverletted iron bedsteads and with snow on the window-sills and ice in the ewers, and at a tremendously uncomfortable (and therefore tremendously good) public school. Roughly speaking, the more appalling and spartan the conditions, the higher the academic standard and the more expensive the school. No nation but the British would understand this and accept it as being quite reasonable.

Readers may, in their sympathetic way, be aware that Devon, hitherto a county of balmy breezes, soothing temperatures and weather conditions that favour almost exotic treats for the eye, such as Torquay's famed palm trees that are practically oriental in their splendour and the begonia-packed flower-beds of Teignmouth (during their brief periods of being unvandalised), has now become almost overnight a prime blizzard area, the first to welcome, if that be the really right verb, the snow and the last to say good-bye to it. What is especially irritating is that Cornwall (old enmities die, as you see, very hard) almost always gets off scot free. Why should Bodmin bask and Dawlish shiver? What has poor old Sidmouth, an outstandingly attractive seaside town, done to fare worse than Newquay?

Within the stately walls of 'Myrtlebank', all richly rose-clad during the summer months, we rely for heat less heavily on fossil fuels, as we now apparently have to call them (no oil tanker driver, unless just about to be certified, would brave my narrow lane), than on the ability of apple trees to, every so often, kick the bucket. Felled and sawn up by my highly valued colleague, Mr Bidder (aged a stalwart 82 and for diligence an example to all), they make the most agreeable and sweet-smelling wood for open fires. Nothing nicer. If there is what is known as 'a good fire going' I am apt to sit up past my normal bed-time (9.30 p.m., with a book) to enjoy it. With only a subdued light in the room, the flickering flames are a constant pleasure to watch. One is wafted back to what was one of the best and simplest of childhood's pleasures – going to sleep by firelight. Heat and happiness. Pat-a-cake biscuits and milk quietly digesting within. A teddy-bear (arm missing) for company. Warmth and security (not, sadly, the experience of many). And a light to keep the bogey-man away. I can only hope that my second childhood (not too far distant now) may hold a few pleasures as sharp.

# *Keep still*

I rather regret the disappearance, in our currently speed-geared lives, of a leisurely form of theatrical entertainment that was popular with Victorians and Edwardians and which lasted on well into the 1920s. I recall as a boy many evenings of delight with my paternal grandmother in the theatre at Colchester, and similar outings to the Alexandra Hall, Ilfracombe (maternal grandfather), and I am referring of course to programmes of *tableaux vivants*. These might be anything from Death of Nelson to Coronation of Elizabeth I and involved a number of persons, keen amateurs all, rigging elaborately up in correct period clothes, usually from Clarksons, and adopting postures to represent, preferably, some well-known painting. They then held their positions as motionlessly as possible, the curtain was raised, they were bathed in footlights and limelights, pink predominating, and a loyal storm of applause greeted them. The length of time that the curtain remained up depended entirely on the extent to which the cast was seen to be wobbling. Items held aloft – Elizabeth's crown, perhaps, or a gladiator's sword bravely brandished and with togaed Roman onlookers wearing scornful expressions and doing a thumbs down – were difficult to keep steady and when these potential wobbles were present one had to look pretty sharp about drinking it all visually in before the curtain swooshed down relentlessly and hid the pictorial treat from sight. There was then a mad scamper backstage to prepare for the next *tableau* ('Ethel, you're standing on my wimple').

Sometimes, the *tableaux vivants* took place before a background of draped curtains and one scene could therefore follow another without too much delay, When Did You Last See Your Father? gliding into Sentence of Death with barely a hiccough, but at Colchester they went in for full sets of scenery and here the waits were longish though the audience were kept

67

on their toes by the sounds of busy activity behind the curtain —
shufflings and bangings and hammerings and thuds and muted
cries of anguish ('The ruddy thing's stuck!'). And being seated
alongside my grandmother was always a pleasure and at
*tableaux vivants* she was constantly trying to identify the
players for, apart from a printed list of appetite-whetting
*tableaux*, no names were provided ('I *think* that Queen Eliza-
beth must have been Mrs Fairfax's younger sister, of whom
we've been hearing so much, and the fallen gladiator was
definitely that new man, Mr Crocker, at Barclays'). I have said
before that our senses of humour ran along parallel and
slightly reprehensible lines and we both greatly enjoyed and
looked out for Signs of Wobble. I remember a merry moment
in a Roman orgy scene (though it certainly wasn't called that
on the programme) when a bunch of grapes held up in a
shaking hand suddenly released one of its nutritious purple
globules which came plopping down into the mouth open
below it. My grandmother shook to such an extent that our
row of seats wobbled too.

One Christmas holidays at Ilfracombe I was pressed into
service and required to take part in one of a series of Scenes
from Dickens. I forget precisely in which one I figured but,
dressed as, what else, a perky lad of 10, I sat at a tea-table while
my mother, voluminously garbed and with a mob-cap, made
to dispense tea from a large brown tea-pot held, perilously,
aloft and at the ready (not a wobble out of her for a full forty
seconds). There were other partakers of tea to be seen motion-
less here and there and you might think that, for a wildly
stage-struck boy, this appearance represented some sort of
exciting theatrical treat. Not at all. I was much put out by
having no words to say, no movements to make. Proper stage
actors didn't just sit there, still and silent, did they? Well then! I
considered myself, odious and spoilt even then, already a
seasoned performer, having appeared before the public as a
mouse, Hiawatha, a French doctor in a farcical frog sketch
called '*Malade, hein?*', and as a Jolly Jack Tar, complete with
hornpipe dance, all of them roles involving speech, movement
and clear diction. I had even secured a laugh in '*Malade, hein?*'
with a piece of business in which I applied my stethoscope to a
lady invalid's chest and did much rolling of the eyes at the
sounds to be heard down it.

In case my recollections of *tableaux vivants* inspire you to get some up on your own account and to begin hunting about for suitable paintings to copy with living figures, let me just sound a warning note. Choice of subject is absolutely vital. For example, Fra Angelico's *The Attempted Martyrdom of SS Cosmas and Damian* (you'll recollect that the flames from their communal stake turned back and attacked their executioners) carries with it a fire risk that not even the Prudential, such a pal in calamity, would care to cover. Then, Turner's *The Petworth Lake at Sunset* cries out for scenic and lighting resources that would certainly have been beyond the range even of Colchester. Why not start quite simply with, perhaps, El Greco's *The Tears of St Peter* for which you will need a bearded player with very large and watery eyes, a tortured expression and a loose-fitting dark blue kimono, chest 42? Then on, possibly, to Picasso's *The Dancers* for which you merely require three angular and deformed ladies, one of whom has got an eye in her chest. I don't think that I would recommend any pictures by Gauguin as so many of his lady subjects were rather absent-minded about putting on clothes, though I dare say that Interflora could manage hibiscus blossoms if asked. Uccello's *The Hunt* rules itself out by demanding 9 hounds, 15 horses and a platoon of bowmen, while Gainsborough's *The Harvest Waggon* isn't going to mean very much without an extremely large and lumpy harvest waggon. However, I can recommend, and particularly in areas boasting a MacFisheries, Raphael's *The Miraculous Draught of Fishes*. The herons, 14 in number, may be omitted, and you will find that, backstage, the fishy smell very soon wears off.

# Murder most foul

My first brush with really serious crime occurred when I was seven years old. We lived in Barnes, then thought of as a village and an attractive and still largely unspoilt near-neighbour to the rather less charming Hammersmith. Our house was in a road called Castelnau, Barnes's main artery and named, or so we imagined, after a French general who had, for once, achieved something. Further up the road lived two friends of mine, a brother and sister called Joan and Boysie (I never knew his real name), aged a ripe eight and nine, and one morning it was discovered, the news spreading like wildfire through our kindergarten, that their house had been burgled the night before.

I had by then started to read *Punch*. The merry illustrated jokes had my father in stitches and when they did not feature slatternly kitchen-maids with wisps of hair all over their foreheads ('Drat them guests!') or amusing social *faux pas* by *nouveaux riches* (collapse of Mr and Mrs Goldhoarder), they were quite often about burglars and so I knew perfectly well what a burglar looked like – burly build, cap, jemmy, mask, dark lantern and a bag labelled SWAG. They arrived on the tick of midnight and were invariably confronted by 'startled householder' in a dressing-gown and waving a poker, upon which they said something appealingly Cockney and witty which always began with 'Nar, 'old on a minute, guv . . .'.

It was all tremendously exciting. The burglar, though obviously not yet at the very summit of his profession, had indeed arrived under cover of darkness and had succeeded in forcing open the pantry window (Joan and Boysie, snoring away in their nursery, hadn't heard a *thing*, little idiots). Reaching in, he had removed some items of plated cutlery and, evidently satisfied with the night's haul, had removed himself too via the garden. And in the garden, thrill upon thrill, he had left, in a flower-bed beneath the window, the impression of a sturdy boot, said to be size 10. My friends' parents, no fools, immediately erected above the telltale footprint a construction of glass to protect it from wind and rain and, thus preserved, to allow the lynx-eyed police to deduce from it the criminal's name and home address (they failed) and bring him speedily to justice. And the affair, complete with smudgy snap of the venue, got into the local paper.

I regret to say that the attitude of Joan and Boysie now became quite insufferable. Socially they were on to a very good thing and they knew it. No Victorian hostess with a lion to parade ('Mr Browning may be looking in later') could have been more unbearably condescending. Invitations to tea showered down like a ticker-tape welcome and were visited on anybody who looked even remotely as though they were going to be properly impressed. Through 'influence' (my nanny was a friend of their nanny) I went several times. The moment the last ginger-snap had disappeared and the ritual 'May we please get down now?' had been said to whichever adult was presiding at the tea-table, Boysie would, elaborately casual, ask 'Care to see the bootmark?'. And out we went into the garden and there, still fully visible among some rather horrid smelling nasturtiums, was the evidence of crime and of the speedy get-away. Then Joan, gracious as could be, would lead an expedition to the pantry so that we could picture the evil and no doubt grimy hand reaching in, the soft clicking of forks and spoons being gathered up, the malevolent eyes glinting.

A few years later I was brought face to face with murder, or so I rated it in my somewhat over-heated imagination. Motoring with my parents to have tea with a great-aunt resident in north Islington, we went bowling up the Camden Road and passed a street called Hilldrop Crescent and I first heard mention, lowered though the voices might be, of somebody called Crippen. And enquiring subsequently here and there, I was able to discover for what reason he was famous. One of the many disadvantages of getting murdered is that, in addition to having to put up with the numerous inconveniences connected with a premature death, the victim almost always sinks away into a complete anonymity. The murderer hogs the limelight: the dead body is nothing. Posterity's favours in the field of fame are lavished on wrong-doers. We may remember that Dr Crippen's friend (found to be, probably correctly, innocent) was Ethel le Neve, and some may recall that his murdered wife was a buxom stage artiste who called herself Belle Elmore, but who could now produce her real name? Though she might call herself 'Cora Turner' when not before her public, her actual name, wisely suppressed, was Kunigunde Mackamotzki.

And it was the epithet 'Crippen' that, a bare three years later, was hurled by an outraged and suspicious landlady at a man called George Joseph Smith after a rather splashy bathroom fatality in her highly respectable Blackpool lodging-house and involving the death of another Mrs Smith. Now who, even if their life, so to speak, depended on it, could name a single one of the ladies who so unwisely tippy-toed up the aisle to wed this lethal bigamist? Deplorably unfair though it may be, they are, alas, mere stage props in this especially sensational melodrama. Mr Smith's method of procedure, for why try anything new when the results were so satisfactory, never varied. With the bride secured and her money made over to him, he hastened out of their furnished rooms and purchased from an ironmonger an enamel bath. Doubtless besotted with his whiskers and winning ways, the ladies seem to have fallen in with his friendly plan to join them, if temporarily, in the room where the bath was set up as he would be useful in carrying up hot water. But with what husbandly wiles did he persuade them to disrobe, step into the filled bath and over-look his continued presence at what should have been a purely private time? Did he possibly suggest to the wife of the moment that she should wash her woman's glory and offer to lend a hand ('Come dear, let me soap your bun')? It was his habit, the deed once done, to hurry to the nearest harmonium and, pedalling vigorously, send out a musical message into the night ('Nearer My God To Thee') that another loved one had perished aquatically.

Whoever claims never to have been morbidly fascinated by murder is almost certainly lying. Even with a bad road accident, it is not away from the distressing and horrifying spectacle that people walk but towards it. Protests of 'I only wanted to see if I could help' are seldom fully accurate. Who can doubt that the House Full boards went up on Christians v Lions nights at the Colosseum? Human nature changes little, if at all, and Messrs J. H. H. Gaute and Robin Odell knew what they were doing when they dreamt up *The Murderers' Who's Who*,

*as he would be useful in carrying up the hot water*

astutely published by Harrap at £8.95 a shudder – a detailed review of the most remarkable murders of the last 150 years, appallingly fully illustrated and utterly not for the squeamish.

Here is the cellar at Hilldrop Crescent where selected portions of Kunigunde found their not very final resting place (she was identified by a piece of abdominal scar tissue). Here is the far from empty trunk which, by sensory means, announced its presence in 1927 in the Charing Cross left-luggage office at a time when, or so it seemed, no such railway office anywhere in the country was considered complete without a dead body or two. There is an electrocution and a guillotining and several corpses (I always understood that such photographs were official ones and forbidden to see a public light of day). A classified index announces place of demise and murder method (blunt instruments tremendously popular down the years). Hopeless to expect, in one's priggish way, any sort of good taste to be displayed in this kind of thing but I would really have thought, mindful of the feelings of parents who are almost certainly still alive, that the photograph might have been suppressed of a friend of Neville George Heath after he had finished with her. Here again, whence and with whose permission come such horrors?

# Pleasantly situated

Strange as it may seem, there were quite a lot of advantages, in which I do not include being on the receiving end of showers of bombs, attached to wartime residence in London. The city was, for one thing, relatively and understandably empty. Few who didn't actually need to remain, remained. One seldom had to stand in tube trains, and buses, fearlessly driven through the worst of the blitzes, had seats. Taxis too circulated dauntlessly in the black-out, together with, I am informed, other conveniences that ply for hire by night. Hitler arranged for everybody, it is true, noisy and disastrous moments but in general a mood of quiet acceptance reigned. There was no need to book a table at a restaurant and, with the cost of a meal limited by law to 5/-, if memory serves, you could eat at upper-crust establishments not normally on your visiting list. Accommodation was cheap and you could stay in hotels well beyond your ordinary peacetime range and thus it was that I put up, on occasion and on leave from elsewhere, at the Ritz, the Savoy and Claridges, though please do not imagine that I say this in any boastful spirit. It could happen to anybody. And there was a further pleasure. Residence in these delightful hotels, all of which were carrying on in a splendidly defiant style, enabled one to offer hot water and baths to friends who, braving the bombs and bangs in private houses or flats, had often had their water or gas cut off, or both, and welcomed a good scrub. If the hotel managements noticed these additional strains on their resources, they were kind enough not to mention it.

Although it was a great enjoyment to stay in the de luxe and above-mentioned establishments, I have had all my life a passion for putting up at every kind of hotel, no matter how humble or run down. There is always something to fascinate one and catch the eye – the proprietress's proudly jutting bosom and careful tones, a fly-blown and faded photograph of Kitchener in a lavatory, the only waiter's soup-stained bags, a bust of Beethoven in the hallway, the splendidly hideous and uncomfortable furnishings in the first-floor drawing-room (Residents Only). There is, too, the happy moment of arrival, the loud coughing to attract attention at the desk, the signing of one's name just below that of Major Tregunter-Jones whom one is later going to meet in the bar ('No old man, this is my shout'), and the receptionist saying, on seeing that you have some luggage to be carried up, 'I'll just ring for Leonard'. A bell peels and after a minute or so of silence and inactivity, the receptionist heaves her top half over the desk, stares into the hotel's hinterland and calls sharply, 'Len!'. I sometimes find myself nowadays in large modern hotels (268 rooms, all with bath) and I note that here it is often assumed at the reception desk that one's stay is going to be paid for, and would to God it were, by some important concern that is holding a convention there ('Excuse me, but are you with Hoggitt and Bumfield or Crowther and Twitch?') and one has hurriedly to deny the flattering suggestion that one is something big in big business and a name to conjure with in the world of jute.

The first London hotel that I ever entered was, as it happens, the Savoy, though it was only for dinner. It was towards the end of the first world war, September 1918, and my parents had decided on what was then called 'a binge', the Zeppelin menace being over and the dreaded Boche about to be on the run. Dinner first and then a theatre. I was eight-years-old and my excitement must have been alarming to behold. A dear old Number 9 bus conveyed us from Barnes to the Strand and we sat in the Savoy restaurant and gazed out over the Thames while we drank some soup or other and ate grilled soles and, of course, ices. And then (and I bless my parents to this day for their choice, and indeed for countless other things) we went to a revue called *Tails Up* at the Comedy Theatre and I got my first sight, though very far from the last, of those two matchless performers, Jack Buchanan and Phyllis Monkman, both great stars whose charm and expertise in song, dance and comic sketch were unsurpassed. One must not, I suppose, raise a scornful lip at the frenzied and displeasing (such dreadful grimaces) antics of some modern musical pop people and I will merely state that in the days of which I speak, stars were proper stars and had earned their stardom the hard way and knew

*No, old man, this is my shout*

their business. And then, six years later, we positively stayed at a hotel, the Tavistock in the very heart of Covent Garden (rattles of carts and bangs and shouts and vegetable smells from 4 a.m. on) and went to another revue, *By-The-Way* at the Apollo with the Hulberts in it, stars indeed.

Then came eight years, on and off, at the imposing Hotel Russell in Russell Square and within spitting distance, if you'll forgive the phrase, of those Bloomsbury figures whom recent and really excessive over-exposure has turned into, for some of us, such appalling bores. I had acquired an Austin Steven, than which no mini is minier, and driving it bravely and inexpertly from Cambridge to London, Southampton Row and the Hotel Russell were the furthest that I dared to penetrate into the capital. It was a splendid piece of luck for me. Solid comfort lay behind those welcoming doors and for 13/6 one had bed and a lavish breakfast suitable for an ex-undergraduate aged 21 (porridge, kippers, egg and bacon and 'can I have some more toast, please?'). A special desk in the hall booked you theatre seats. Taxis could be whistled up from outside. This was, one felt, the life and, dressed up to what I assumed to be the nines, one went the pace I can tell you. How sadly ludicrous one must have looked and how disagreeably demanding one must have seemed to the hotel servants.

We now have the reactions to guests of at least one such hotel servant in Anthony Masters' *Inside Marbled Halls* (Sidgwick & Jackson, £7.95), a pleasing biography of Mary Shiffer from Dublin who arrived at the Hyde Park Hotel in 1916 and who stayed for nearly 60 years. Shunting between the still-room and the restaurant and endlessly cutting bread-and-butter, she swiftly became a loved 'character' and it was fashionable for royalty and lesser persons to drop in on her for a chat (at a silver wedding party, she danced the conga with George VI). The royal entrance (on the Park) had limited accommodation and possessed no ladies' lavatory and Queen Mary had, on her visits, to make do with a commode to which a curtseying Mary conducted her as and when necessary. You never knew who might not be staying. One minute it was Gustav of Sweden, and the next Rico of Denmark. The Sultan of Zanzibar arrived with, among other companions, 12 goats who had to be milked on the first floor and who forgot themselves all over everywhere (something to do with his religion, I dare say). There was Kosygin's visit when the Russian Secret Service checked everything in sight, 'even my coffee urn. I was furious'. And there were the second world war and unexploded bombs and victory celebrations. How splendid of Mr Masters to preserve for us the joyous pronouncement put out by the Board of Trade on 7 May 1945:

Until the end of May you may buy cotton bunting without coupons, as long as it is red, white or blue and does not cost more than one and three a square yard.

Earning originally £2 a month, and firmly referring to Italian waiters as Macaronis, Mary's crisp vignettes are illuminating. Queen Mary ('She never said anything that wasn't ordinary'). Evelyn Waugh ('Moody and often very rude'). Bette Davis ('Looking very smouldering'). Lady Docker ('She had a kind of child-like wonder'). Débutantes' balls ('A cattle market in full swing'). Then there was Rosa Lewis ('That God-awful woman'), apt to breeze up to ancient dukes with a merry cry of 'How's the old water works these days?'.

Mary (now dead, alas) finally retired at the age of 85, glad to have been of service ('I helped them all, didn't I? I helped them all'). I doubt if they make them like that any more. 'This brand has now been discontinued.'

# *I believe*

You will recall that in *Alice Through the Looking-Glass*, the Queen boasted that when she was young she had been able to believe as many as six impossible things before breakfast, a feat well beyond the range of those of us who are far from at our best until coffee, kippers and toast have gone comfortingly down the red lane. Two rather interesting and, to me, ticklesome facts or 'things' have recently come my way, one of which, though not absolutely impossible to believe, must certainly rank in most minds as being highly improbable. I say 'improbable' rather daringly and, possibly, impertinently because the source of the information, and it is historical information, is a very distinguished historian and writer, none other than Sir Steven Runciman. He has been heard to state that, on the death of Louis XIV, the Sun King mainly resident at Versailles, his heart was carefully and reverently removed and stored away in a bejewelled box. Many years later (can it have been perhaps during the Revolution when kings, or parts of kings, were not popular?), it found its way to England, by now rather reduced in size, and much later still it was decided to exhibit this fascinating relic at some august and high-powered gathering (a sprinkling of professors, dons, ministers, ambassadors and the more successful type of clergyman) in London – not exactly a cheese-and-wine 'do' but with something for the guests to sip. The heart was taken from its box and placed upon a silver salver for all to see and marvel at, and there it remained until a short-sighted bishop, salivating for another canapé, mistook it for a cocktail dainty, scooped it up and gobbled it down. True or false?' It's up to you.

I shall return to my other 'thing' shortly, just turning aside for a moment to mention the fact that the late Miss Edna Ferber, a formidable American lady novelist and the provider, to the benefit of all of us, of such literary treats as *Show Boat* and *Saratoga Trunk*, was kindly inspired one day to give in her New York apartment a big welcome to a visiting English lady novelist of, then, considerable fame and whom, though now alas dead too, I will call Miss G. I use the letter G rather than the customary X because G stands for greedy and gluttonous and gigantic and gawky and gifted and she was all of those. Miss Ferber, deciding that a tea-party for twelve would be the ideal thing, summoned her most suitable Anglophile friends, ordered cakes and buns galore, got out her best china and laid (rather prissily and fussily some of us might consider) upon each of the guest's plates a small mat or, repulsive word, doily of exquisitely light and filmy Brussels lace and of which she possessed, fortunately, just a dozen so that there was one for each. The guests arrived and Miss G arrived and, with appetite doubtless sharpened by the keen New York air, despatched every eatable that came her way, choking a little from time to time. The guests left and Miss G left and the hostess, tidying up, gathered together her doilies and found to her dismay that there were only eleven of them, the one on Miss G's plate having gone missing. Yes indeed. It had evidently got caught up in a slice of angel cake and had been engulfed along with it. Some stomachs can digest just anything. True or false? True, as it happens, and my informant was Miss Ferber herself, still very rattled at what she considered to be this unreasonable demand made upon her nutritional resources.

Being rather greedy too, I do not have much time for those who, claiming to be far above such mundane matters, state that they seldom 'notice' what they are eating and are quite prepared to make their guests suffer along with them. Food is about the only pleasure that continues, more or less unchanged, from the cradle to the grave and should be treated with proper respect. I do not approve of those who are not much prepared to bother. In Devon I was once the periodical guest at lunch or dinner of a widowed lady called Millie to whom we were all deeply devoted, and just as well perhaps for her food was of a really sensationally disgusting nature – gravy with blobs of fat swimming about, mint sauce with no sugar in it, boiled potatoes that crunched crisply in the mouth, and undercooked roast shoulders that squeaked protestingly when carved. There was, somewhere in the hinterland, a cook called Bessie and, by way of summoning us to the table, Millie invariably said 'Now, dears, let's go and see what the gallant Bessie has given us.'

Somebody among our friends advanced the theory that Millie's taste buds had long since atrophied and no dissentient voices were heard. Determined to put the matter to the test, we hatched a plan. This consisted of a telephone call made by an accomplice during dinner and which would remove Millie momentarily from the table. We then got busy. The pudding course had been reached and into the soggy folds of trifle upon her plate we inserted layers of mustard, pepper and salt, but Millie, returning, got it all down in a trice and then gave a glad cry of 'Jolly good! Anybody game to join me in another spoonful?' Unkind of us, perhaps.

But about my other fact (see para. 1) there can be no possible salmon-and-trout (Cockney rhyming slang for we are now back again in London) as the information comes from too many totally reliable sources. Though I have already mentioned it in another periodical, I repeat it here for the benefit of NS readers and it concerns the soft background music provided by a military band (a Guards one for a certainty) while Her Majesty is presiding at an investiture and handing out gongs and dubbing some of her worthier (usually) subjects. Sometimes the music is charmingly suitable. Sir Noël Coward was favoured with 'Clair de Lune', the moon in this case clearly ranking as a heavenly body and doing service as a 'star'. But now a kind correspondent, recently present at the Palace while his sister was being decorated, writes to tell me that Her Majesty made her entrance to the tuneful strains of 'Bess, you is my woman now', a number belonging, one would have thought, solely to the Duke of Edinburgh, and in a private capacity at that. She exited on this occasion to 'The Entry of the Gladiators' which, with its reference to the beginning rather than to the end of a circus, seems to have been a mysterious choice indeed. There have been other oddities. When Lord Olivier first became Sir Laurence it was to 'The Donkey's Serenade'. Anna Neagle bobbed about and became Dame Anna to 'Hello Dolly', while Daphne du Maurier was damed to the merry accompaniment of 'A Life on the Ocean Wave.'

Choosing fitting musical accompaniments for this or that occasion is a tricky business and I have recently been keeping tabs, as they say, on the music that is put out to go with that

ITV notice regretting the temporary absence of telly program-
mes and at which a million people are said to sit and stare,
presumably, I thought at first, in the wild hopes that the box
would suddenly flood with light and be once more brightly
radiant with 'Crossroads' and the heart-stopping shocks and
joys of 'This Is Your Life' ('. . . and here's your ninety-year old
Auntie Nellie, not in Winnipeg as you thought, but flown here
to be with us this evening . . .' followed by some unintelligible
nonagenarian croakings and everybody having a good blub).
But it is now clear to me why these million devoted viewers sit.
They are not so much staring as listening. The music is one
long pleasure. The stuff chosen for the BBC 1 Test Card is
pretty lightweight – pop and Eric Coates and so on. BBC 2's
Test Card is only marginally better. But the ITV 'Sorry' notice
has been accompanied throughout by only the very best in
what we must call classical music – Mozart and Beethoven and
Haydn and so on. One would have expected the loudest of
pop, given to us by those groups with the not immediately
attractive names (is there one called 'Sludge'? I offer it, any-
way). But not a bit of it. Distinguished orchestras scrape and
blow. Famous pianists thunder out concertos while a million
people sit entranced. Full marks to somebody.

# *Cheese it, sly-boots!*

Having informed the public, and probably to excess, that I recently achieved my allotted span of years and am now at risk from the Grim Reaper, I have been much cheered by a kind friend who encouraged me to press cheerfully on by telling me of a really very very ancient male American of his acquaintance who was heard one day wistfully murmuring 'Oh to be eighty again!' Octogenarianism is, therefore, now my target. A further encouragement was provided the other day in this, our Devon geriatric belt, by the realisation at a delightful tea-party given by my dear old Cousin Madge (Earl Grey, cucumber sandwiches, maids of honour and a light sponge) that I was by far the youngest person present. Indeed, so great was the gap between myself and the next person up (88) that I felt I ought, for it was a summery day, to be wearing a floppy felt sun-hat and gray flannel shorts held up by a snake-clasp belt in my prep school colours (a patriotic red, white and blue).

Looking back as, in old age, one constantly does, it being a less agitating and jollier occupation than looking forwards, I find that the mists of time have kindly obliterated, more or less, any depressing and humiliating incidents that took place (being sick in almost anything that moved, the No. 9 bus particularly) and only the happy and memorable and enjoyable moments remain – childhood picnics in Richmond Park and hide-and-seek among the ferns, the fun of bathing in rough Ilfracombe seas, the discovery of the works of Miss Angela Brazil, one's first oyster, the joy of shared laughter (one of Life's major boons), and matinée after matinée. I have only one real regret (apart from the nagging feeling that one let slip, and on many occasions, a chance of doing a kindness) and that is that in my last year at Cambridge I did not read English rather than peg on, slackly though I did it, with foreign lingos of which I had had a sufficiency, for I had already 'done' French, more or less, and got little comfort from the, to me, arid wastes of German literature. Or, failing English, why had I not done a brisk year of another and different foreign tongue?

Ah yes, but which? It would certainly not have been Dutch. There are said to be languages where a simple thing like saying 'Good morning; nice day' is so complicated and takes such a while that by the time you have got the whole thing out, the person addressed is long since out of earshot. This appears to be one of the very few failings that cannot be laid at the door *(het deur)* of the Dutch. Curt explosions of sound are rather more their line: 'uncles' come out as *ooms* and 'Don't!' seems to be just *Au!*, pronounced I know not how, and so presumably 'Don't, uncle!' is *Au, oom!* I ask you! My chief quarrel with Dutch, however, is that it is deliberately misleading. For example, if invited to *Het koffiedrinken*, who in their senses would imagine that it meant anything but an ordinary mid-morning 'elevenses', as some phrase it, with coffee, soggy Dutch pastries and, possibly, slices of Gouda, and with conversation limited to the advantages, if any, of wearing clogs, and the wind/energy ratio, or whatever, of windmills. But not a bit of it. *Het koffiedrinken* means lunch. Could anything be more purposely muddling?

Then there is the word, if such it can be called, which is spoken in a rising and interrogative tone and means 'isn't it?' and is written *Hè*, as in 'this soused herring tastes simply filthy, *hè*'. Despite the fact that the Dutch race is on the whole pretty solidly built, from the House of Orange down, they go in quite a lot for playful diminutives. One would have settled, more or less, for *boom* meaning tree, but no, there has to be a 'little tree' and it is *boompje*. The dreadful word 'wifey' comes out as *vrouwtje*. Small drawers (and there seems to be no means of knowing whether wooden drawers are intended, or whether we are in the garment world) appear to be *laatje*. When I add that *kip* seems to mean chicken, *fiets* is bicycle and *boterham* is merely 'slice of bread and butter' and with not a trace of ham to it, you can see how terribly on your guard you must be. Any language in which 'frog' comes out as *Kikker* is simply not to be trusted.

Our own splendidly rich tongue, plain sailing though it may be for us natives as we rattle it effortlessly off, seems to provide a trap or two for foreigners and there has recently come my way a conversation manual for those Italians who are planning a daring trip to our shores (and I personally have decided to overlook the fact that the name of the booklet's Torino compiler and publisher is, regrettably, F. Casanova, nor am I even going to wonder for one moment what that F might stand for). The compiler of this fine feast of English conversational possibilities is very strong on, so to speak, a balanced diet of pain and pleasure, of sunshine and shadow. Joys and calamities intermingle, as they do so freely in the warp and woof of life. Thus, 'The sun is very hot' is closely followed by 'We shall soon have snow'. Then, friendly comments such as 'Look, here comes Miss Mary!' and 'May I introduce Mrs Emily?' rapidly give way to 'My watch has stopped' and 'Be Quiet!'

I am not too sure how popular our Italian is going to be as he travels, by rail or road, from place to place. Helpful though British Rail can often be, cries of 'Give me a pillow, please' and 'Waiter, bring me a ham sandwich!' are, even if heard, not going to strike a very chummy or productive note on the 8.41 a.m. to Worthing, ready though the traveller may be to claim his rights ('Pardon me, this is my seat'). Endless luggage mishaps are, quite rightly, envisaged, and amid a plethora of lost umbrellas, waterproofs, brief-cases and bags, there is a short sharp wail of 'My trunk is missing, and my pocketbook has been stolen!' Any garage proprietor who chances to own a garage on the London to Brighton road ('How many miles is it to Reigate? Is the way slippery?') had better consider himself warned of the approach of an Italian car with almost everything wrong with it, and he will soon discover just what. 'Wash the car. The engine is not working properly – there is a diminution of power. You must change the bush of the engine, register the tappets and grind the valves. Test the electric wiring and check the level of oil in the differential. A tyre needs repairing. Is your garage heated?' The generally gloomy tone of this section is nowhere more in evidence than in the preparation for road accidents *(Incidenti di strada)*. 'Your car has crushed one of my wings! My car is smashed and it is your fault! Give me your driving licence! I came in from your left and so I had the precedence. This gets my goat!'

It is, as we know from past experience, in the treacherous field of slang that most foreigners fall flat on their faces and one wonders how recently and for how long F. Casanova graced our island. The English owner of the car which crushed an Italian wing will not, as he expostulates, be much cheered by saucy ripostes of 'Cheese it!' and 'Silence, sly-boots!' and 'Come off it, old horse!', not to speak of 'You're a rum'un'. Nor is nowadays the word 'bobbery' in really constant use (to save you hastening to your Chambers, it is given as meaning 'a noisy row' – row to rhyme with bough, I take it). Two of the phrases supplied are new to me: 'To come to the gutter' and 'To cut it fat' seem to make no sense at all, but then I lead a rather sheltered life and seldom get out, and for all I know what is known as *tout Londres* may be constantly cutting it fat. How flattered, I ask myself, would Miss Mary be (we have already met her in the chatty 'Look, here comes Miss Mary'), to hear a sotto voce mutter of 'she's a nice little bit of goods'. Alas, the word 'nose-rag' for handkerchief is very far from pleasing, and does not benefit from finding itself among odd companions ('I say, I'm putting on my glad rags, so lend me a nose-rag and make it snappy'). One can only be thankful that F. Casanova has not included a section ('Come, Miss Mary, let me caress your chest') featuring his namesake's amorous activities.

# Men's sauna

There are, as is obvious, enormous advantages connected with being able to live in the depths of the country, and I do not only speak scenically and gastronomically (there's nothing like a Devonian new-laid egg and my neighbour's free-range chickens, pleasingly dotty-looking birds, are so joyously free-range that they consider themselves to be welcome everywhere, even in church, and they occasionally deposit a speckled and oval tribute among my dahlias while passing through on their way to Matins). Remoteness provides a protection against many of Life's problems and against the difficulties that agitate large communities and tear the world apart, and prominent among the problems that in no way touch us here at Appleton is that of nude bathing.

Appleton, though a real feast for the eyes and chock-a-block with valuable activity (a Jumble Sale is 'on' at the village hall as I write) is, quite frankly, no centre for bathing, draped or otherwise. Swiftly-moving and icy-cold streams from Dartmoor dash through it on their way down to the Teign river in the valley below. Here and there a small and muddy pond forms, paddled in in hot weather by cows and sipped at by sheep. This is not bathing country, apart from the great local blessing of the Bultitudes' spacious pool, so thoughtfully made available to all and sundry throughout the year. Elegant Giles and Bunty lead the revels before, during and after the dip, with 'Who's for a noggin?' from Giles at one end of the *piscine*, a cheery invitation echoed by 'How's about a snifter?' from Bunty at the other. How extraordinarily kind and generous such merry extroverts almost always are.

Nobody would dream of assaulting the Bultitude pool with no clothes on. Visitors not expecting to plunge are catered for in the changing-rooms where Giles supplies a row of what he refers to as 'spare bum-bags'. I myself make use in their pool of my own cherished pair of swimming-trunks which I purchased many years ago now in, of course, the Army & Navy Stores in London's Victoria Street. They were in a tasteful black and white design, now faded to grey, and they have taken with me to the waters in a wide variety of places. Together we have enjoyed Ibiza (so splendid for schnorkeling), the Gulf of Mexico (in company with about a million pelicans), a private pool in Wisconsin (shared with mosquitoes and chipmunks), Barbados (can there be more marvellous bathing anywhere in the world?), and year after happy year at Amalfi (just round the corner from Naples and on the Gulf of Salerno). My sturdy and tremendously hard-wearing trunks have a sort of white inner lining fashioned from some soft and rather elastic material which has stood splendidly up to all the calls made upon it. And it gives me an enormous advantage over other swimmers. If, when ready for the briny, I choose to enter the water by holding my nose and then jumping in off a rock (a diving board would be rather too showy and modesty forbids it), the lining fills, as I zoom downwards, with air and provides me with my own personal flotation chambers, a bodily feature which, as delightful David Attenborough kept on pointing out in that splendid TV series, few aquatic animals can afford to be without. If I dive in, the same thing occurs and a comforting belt of air held captive round my middle ensures a really quite unusual buoyancy. Perched up in the water is what I am and able to peer about and drink in the other bathers. Incidentally, I like to think of my dive as being of the swallow variety but I have learnt, after performing it, to stay under water for as long as possible (not easy, with my flotations). By the time I surface, those who were sunbathing near me at the moment of impact have usually stopped swearing and dabbing at themselves with towels, and the most turbulent of the waves caused by my splash have subsided.

In none of the resorts that I have mentioned above have I ever seen a suggestion of nude bathing, that subject that is currently exercising so many keen minds in modish centres along our south coast where, so icy and appalling is the condition of the English Channel water (for four years I bathed regularly in the Solent and so I know what I am talking about), that I would have thought that it was a case of the more clothes the better. Some newspapers have even had lead articles upon the matter and, to demonstrate how jolly their approach is,

*I like to think of my dive as being of the swallow variety*

have headed them 'Strip Ahoy!' Well, if people wish to bathe as God, if on rather an off day, made them, why on earth shouldn't they? I can see no moral objection, though aesthetic ones are two a penny. As everybody must know by now, the more clothes that are removed from the average human body, the less appetising it becomes as a spectacle. The final nude state is, in most cases, very far from pleasing to the eye. So much that shouldn't really wobble, wobbles. As Sir Robert Helpmann so wisely said when discussing the pros and cons of ballet performed in the nude, 'not everything stops when the music stops.'

Nudity and countless other bodily matters are fully examined in the *Encyclopaedia of Natural Health and Healing* (Kaye & Ward, £6.25), the work of Mr Harvey Day, born in Bangladesh, interested 'in yoga and the occult' and at one point rather surprisingly an engineer with the Eastern Bengal

Railway before settling for dietetics, health and cookery. His book is a richly stuffed bran-tub of widely assorted information, though he begs readers (as indeed and most emphatically do I) to 'consult with their physician' before bringing any of the suggested remedies and specifics into play. Especially striking are the claims that he makes for the common or garden (indeed) stinging nettles. Not a particle of them need be wasted. Boil the top four inches and hey presto, a spinach-substitute is to hand. Drain off the water and use it as stock (good for slimmers). Nettle poultices relieve pain. Boiled nettle water puts paid to worms (species not stated). Make a fragrant tea from nettle roots and say farewell to haemorrhage of the, pardon me, urinary organs. Nettle water is A1 as a hair tonic, restoring its natural colour and curing dandruff (boil the leaves in vinegar and give that scalp a real sousing). Pressed nettle juice is tip-top for constipation. Nettle seeds, steeped in wine, are death to ague. A bunch of nettles hung up in the larder will discourage flies. In 1917, the wily Hun, running short of basics, made socks, greatcoats and tarpaulins from nettles. Personally, I'm going out into the orchard this very moment to gather a great armful of the lovely things. Does one *knit* them to make socks? Ouch!

Oddities abound. There was the sad case of Basil Brown, with a PhD in chemistry, who in 1974 and in ten days swallowed carrot juice containing 70 million units of vitamin A because he thought it would be good for him. He turned bright yellow and passed rapidly away from vitamin poisoning. Hearing that wheat germ and honey improve sexual performances, the inscrutable Japanese bought up honey in such vast quantities that they sent the price up sky-high, though to what extent their home lives were improved is not stated. I am glad to say that Mr Hay speaks up warmly for the virtues of alcohol ('It soothes the anxious mind and is an aid to sociability' – as good an excuse as any). Bananas are a mild laxative. Cleopatra often took 69 (odd number to choose) asses' milk baths a day. Ivan the Terrible was cured of gout by bee stings, which also improved the arthritis of the above-mentioned R. Helpmann ('Now I can dance for hours and hours'). If pushed for an aperient, why not fall back on the humble beetroot? If you were to ban white sugar altogether and halve the amount of salt eaten, many diseases would disappear.

A final tip, and please don't blame me if it doesn't work, though I can hardly think that any damage to the system will result. It is a cure that has been widely scoffed at but Mr Hay was, appropriately enough, cured of hay fever (a martyr to it for 25 years) by chewing honeycomb. But not, as the song has it, 'when the bee's at home'.

# Manly little lads

Those of us who spend our waking hours and earn a sort of living by struggling to string words together in what one hopes to be a palatable and ea-si-ly ass-i-mi-la-ted fashion, find all too little time for reading the efforts of brother pens, dead or alive, who too have struggled and strung. Many is the long day since I have been able to run my eye along the three thousand or so books that, row upon dusty row, grace the walls of 'Myrtlebank' and, tugging out here a treasured Evelyn Waugh (*Scoop*, possibly) and there an early Stella Gibbons (*Bassett*, perhaps), re-live happy hours in the hammock with an apple and when the world was young. When I am really old and gray, and it will be any minute now, I would like to re-read nearly all of Dickens (I've never been able to get along very well with Pickwick) for to me he is, squalor, slop and all, the Master, or rather the Joint-Master for he must budge over and make room on the pedestal for P. G. Wodehouse. In both cases, and as with Shakespeare, the sheer volume of the words provided is breathtaking, though one is not here judging by volume.

My parents were what is known as Great Readers and encouraged one all along the line, though my father tended to stick to Dickens, working steadily through his collected edition and, on completing it, starting, like the Forth Bridge painters, at the beginning again. But my mother was more adventuresome (her reading of Aldous Huxley was locally considered to be very dashing) and when we lived in Berkshire, hardly a week passed without her saying 'Do remind me to go to Boots tomorrow'. For those who today only associate Boots with toothpaste and what now seem to be called Toiletries, Boots Library, coupled with the Times Library (though here the books came by post), was the great literary stand-by of country dwellers in the days before the burgeoning of our excellent county libraries and those splendid travelling ones.

Boots librarians were invariably charming and helpful and often bore unusual names – Miss Foljambe, Miss Plenderleith, Miss Battersby. They sometimes aided one to jump the queue for a currently popular volume, and 'Get Miss Foljambe to sit on it for you' was a modish phrase among booklovers.

At school too and when I was young, reading was much encouraged. Apart from anything else, it kept one quiet and the authorities did not, wisely enough, ban this book or that as being unsuitable. I remember a happy moment when a boy called Morden returned to school with a sensational novel, filched from home, in which the heroine's name was 'Flame' and one of the chapters ended with the dramatic words, spoken by a male member of the cast, 'Flame, lie still!' Some of the more innocent boys thought this must mean that Flame, rather a vigorous girl as I recall, was about to jump up and get herself ready for badminton, but the precocious know-alls among whom I defiantly numbered myself, realised that the gentleman concerned was about to do something physical that would benefit from Flame abandoning all thought of badminton for the time being and remaining relatively motionless for once. Such books were, however and just as well, rare in our lives and for the rest it was the well-thumbed works of Percy F. Westerman, Sapper, Buchan, P. C. Wren, Dornford Yates, Scott and the excessively wholesome yarns of George Alfred Henty (one of the few authors to die on his own yacht in Weymouth harbour), his proud and principal publishers, Blackie, revealing in 1950 that up to then 25 million copies of his books had been eagerly snapped up by the public.

What a jolly surprise it can be when names, famous in other contexts, pop up as fictional ones in books. Who can forget that in Angela Brazil's *A Patriotic Schoolgirl* (it is from her middle period and when she was at the very height of her great powers), by far the naughtiest girl in the school is called Marjorie Anderson, the name of one of the most distinguished and pleasing *commères* of the entirely admirable 'Woman's Hour' on the wireless. Then wasn't it Richard Usborne, brilliant authority on the works of Wodehouse and others, who, digging and delving, discovered that in a cricket match in one of the Master's early school stories, the captains of the opposing teams were called Burgess and Maclean. In this respect, Henty does not let us down. In his *True to the Old Flag* we kick off in Massachusetts at the time of the American War of

Independence and the English boy here is sent off to Lake Huron to learn Indian fighting and woodcraft, prior to being a scout with an irregular force and doing fine work at the battle of Bunker's Hill. He then rescues two girls kidnapped by the Iroquois and I expect you'll want to know the name of this sturdy little chap. It is Harold Wilson. And there is in *Through Three Campaigns* a passage with modern overtones that strikes an altogether less cheerful note. 'When Blunt fell, it was the most natural thing in the world that I should go and pick him up, and I did so almost mechanically.' The speaker and performer of this noble act is a war hero, Captain Bullen, VC.

A splendid new life of Henty, *Held Fast for England* (Hamish Hamilton, £8.95), tells us all we wanted to know but hardly dared to ask (in his books, the constant repetition of the word 'lad', usually such an emotional give-away – look at Housman – had led one to fear the presence of an etiolated and wonky cleric). Not at all. This pipe-smoking and bearded newspaper correspondent who turned the scales at seventeen stone, invented an uncapsizable boat which amazed one and all by its ability to capsize, and eventually married his housekeeper, a Miss Elizabeth Keylock (such a suitable and reliable name for one of her profession) was normal as blueberry pie. He was also Chief Brave of the Wigwam, a small dining club which held cultural evenings and we must be careful what we say about him or we shall be pounced on by members of the Henty Society, formed in 1977 to keep the memory green, or whatever.

Arriving, a somewhat sickly boy, at Westminster School in 1846 and recklessly announcing that he wrote poetry and was fond of flowers, Henty had rapidly to learn boxing to protect himself and acquired the admiration for straight lefts that never deserted either him or his young heroes. At Cambridge and at Caius he pressed on with fisticuffs, learnt to wrestle (well, one never knew), rowed for the college eight and, in between whiles, read Classics. And so into journalism and, with the Crimean War in full and convenient action, as a military and war correspondent, flashing wildly from conflict to conflict. He was among Garibaldi's camp-followers, bobbed up in Russia for the Turkoman War, popped over to the Gold Coast for the Ashanti Campaign, nipped back to Serbia just in time for the Turco-Serbian War, and then it was up and away on the Abyssinian expedition with Napier, after which his health broke down, to the total astonishment of very few.

The Henty stories are rich in exciting historical backgrounds and, after a healthy few years at a public school (Cheltenham is popular, ditto Rugby, and there is at least one Etonian), the heroes tend to be appointed to the staffs of leaders such as Wolfe, Wellington, Turenne and Frederick the Great. Hearty Christianity was the line, with a prayer here and a straight left there, and with muscles preferably knotted and figures sinewy. Not too many brains, mind, and although the manly lads are always described as being merry as can be and full of japes and pranks, one hardly goes to Henty for laughs. Indeed, sober seriousness is everywhere to be seen and nowhere more so than in *Condemned as a Nihilist* ('The Story of Escape from Siberia') where the hero, Godfrey, fights the prison bully ('This fellow has been a nuisance in the ward') and knocks him out with, guess what, a straight left, prior to escaping down, apparently, the River Ob accompanied by a Russian called Luka who, poor chap, gets lectured about God, radicalism, women in politics, flogging, Russia and anything else that happens to cross his, or Henty's, mind. They land up eventually in a remote part of north Norway and serve them right. A fine read, indeed, but it gets 0 out of 10 for fun.

# But for the grace of God

I have written before in these pages of the relief of not owning smartyboots possessions such as yachts, barbecues, floodlit patios, vast cars, split-level dwellings, roomfuls of modern 'gear', penthouse suites and heated open-air pools (always full of leaves and other foreign matter, despite all that scoop, scoop) and I suppose it's nothing but self-satisfaction and smugness that make one pleased with one's lot and utterly content not to have been almost anybody else you may care to mention in history's pages. How very agitating to have been, say, either Nelson or Wellington, with all eyes on you and the country's fate in your tiny trembling hands. How very worrying too to have been anyone with a Call or Cause and in particular Joan of Arc, heroine of a prize-winning entry in the NS black joke competition ('How do you like your steak, Joan?'). But, in a strong field, I think I would least of all have cared to be almost anybody featured in the flowing poetical works of the American versifier known to us as Henry Wadsworth Longfellow.

Wadsworth, I'm sorry to say, was given to spreading himself. Wadsworth's clever pen tended to run on. The complete works, given to us by the Oxford University Press (no strangers to pens that run on) in the 1917 edition, comprises 848 pages, and an average page, taken from a lowering and interminable piece called 'The Courtship of Miles Standish' contains about 450 words. So, when all is said and done, Longfellow presented the world with a cool 380,000 words or so of relentless poetry, and that is really an awful lot of words. And apart from this depressing lavishness, the titles of some of the poems hardly raise our spirits – 'The Lunatic Girl', 'Dirge over a Nameless Grave', 'The Slave in the Dismal Swamp', 'Seaweed', 'Resignation' (to the will of God, rather than from the golf club), 'Weariness', 'Death of Archbishop Turpin', and 'The

Jewish Cemetery at Newport'. And the personages that infest these gems are little better.

Take, for example, the young man in the famous party piece, 'Excelsior', a word meaning 'higher still' and one which has immortalised Longfellow in *Chambers*. Despite expert local advice and solemn warnings, the youth, who was evidently a foreigner, walked, as you'll recall, straight up a mountain side by night in the Alps (one pictures the young hothead in flimsy *après-ski* kit) and pays the extreme penalty exacted by Jack Frost, getting frozen stiff as a poker and dead as a doornail. His climb was hardly made easy by his insistence on bearing with him a banner with the strange device 'Excelsior'. The banner would offer considerable wind resistance and make for heavy going, and all this with weather conditions pointing to about 8 on the Beaufort Scale (mild gale). In addition, the pious monks of St Bernard, startled by the to them meaningless cry of 'Excelsior' as they trooped out, sleepy-eyed, to attend early service ('*Qu'est-ce que c'est que ça?*'), were put to considerable trouble, having to load up a St Bernard dog with a minicask of brandy, push its reluctant body out into the snow, and tell it to start smelling.

Well then, almost anybody afloat in a Longfellow poem has reason to regret the fact. The good ship *Hesperus* was only one of several vividly described wrecks, but of course this one is especially heart-rending because of the presence on board of the captain's little daughter (no name is given. What can it have been? Dawn? Tracy? Cindy-Lou?), an enchanting and understandably timorous blue-eyed mite, rightly apt to clasp her hands in prayer when things are getting dicey. Of the captain's selfishness in taking her with him on the schooner I can hardly bring myself to speak. What is more, it is night time and snowing, clouds have obscured the moon, there's been a warning of Hurricane Hannah and the child should long since have been home and in bed and getting itself outside a glass of Grade A milk and a liberal handful of cookies. However, down they all sink to the ocean floor and find themselves with countless others, notably the entire crew of the *Cumberland*, Sir Humphrey Gilbert (who discovered, I hardly need to remind you, Newfoundland), and almost the whole of the French fleet of 1746. And before we leave this painful subject, let me censure our poet for heartlessness in the relish with which he describes the violent seas that downed the *Hesperus*.

*pushed its reluctant body out into the snow*

'Ho! Ho! the breakers roared!', he writes. Whatever interpretation you may put on 'Ho! Ho!', the words allied to the verb 'roar' ('*How* we all roared!') are most unfortunate and imply derisive laughter.

There is insufficient space here for me to dwell on the many disadvantages of being the devout and black-eyed Evangeline in a piece of 1395 lines, sensibly entitled 'Evangeline', for Hiawatha calls, though not very enticingly. I have never, thank God, been in a wigwam but the inconveniences are fully imaginable – smells, smoke, gloom and woefully inadequate 'toilet' arrangements. There was the added difficulty for Hiawatha in his boyhood and at his prep school of having to answer the age-old question, 'I say, what does your pater do?', with the information that his pater was the West Wind, which just blew from time to time. Ya, boo!

Further facts invite further mockery – a mother, deserted and dead, and a ghastly old wrinkled granny called Nokomis (a daughter of the moon, apparently), who lives by the sea amid talkative pine-trees which keep on saying 'Minne-wawa!'. And indeed Hiawatha's baby tongue has to lisp its way round the most frightful *Call My Bluff* words, such as Sheshebwug (ducks), Waymukkwuna (caterpillars), Be-mahgut (vines), Kuntassoo (plum-stones) and Okahahwis (herrings). In addition all the food sounds pretty off-putting and the best that Nokomis can scare up for the feast after Hiawatha's marriage to Laughing Water is sturgeon (no sign of the roes), pike (caught, heaven knows how, and cooked by Nokomis herself), pemican, buffalo marrow, bison hump and, as the sole starchy item, a little wild rice. This unbalanced and thoroughly over-proteined treat was followed by a cabaret performance given by the fully resistible Pau-Puk-Keewis, very overdressed for the occasion in a doeskin shirt trimmed with ermine and with inserted panels of wampum, dearskin leg-gings hemmed with hedgehog quills, beaded mules, and with the whole rig covered in swan's down and fox furs, complete with a feathered fan which he vigorously flapped, and with his shoulder-length hair 'parted like a woman's'. Oh dear! The sooner we can get that one out of the wigwam and onto the psychiatrist's couch the better. And I'm not too sure that that doesn't go for Wadsworth too.

# Mon Dieu!

There are a number of reasons why 'Myrtlebank' does not rely for its heating upon fossil fuels, to use the currently modish words for oil. There is, for one thing, the expense. There is what may be going to happen in The Gulf (nastinesses, and cries of 'Bags I!'). There would have to be, for another thing, an unsightly oil tank dumped down somewhere on my premises, doubtless destroying a pleasing vista of, perhaps, the roof of one of the village shops, its gracious outlines partly visible through a rather overgrown mahonia. There is also the fact that 'Myrtlebank' lies at the foot of a steep and extremely narrow lane down which a motor oil tanker would hardly dare ('No can do, mate') to venture. And having been present, and feeling not unlike the Great Architect in the sky Himself, when stately 'Myrtlebank' was being created from three ancient and, at the time, condemned mill workers' cottages, and having stood by when, in four places, openings for doors were being driven through stone walls five feet thick, I really could not face again the dust and confusion involved in the installation of pipes to carry the oil or the hot water or whatever.

Do we then in winter freeze, you enquire in your solicitous manner, hurriedly deciding not to ask to come and stay? No we do not. Instant heat is kindly provided by SWEB, our South Western Electricity Board and a widely admired body who will cheerfully bankrupt us all in a year or so, and the heat is disseminated by convectors which disgorge warm air at the click of a switch. And in our two large main rooms, both the very last word in luxi-living, there are open fires, than which few things are cosier and which, as regards wood, are supplied by arboreal fatalities in my spacious grounds that surround the dwelling – with here a laburnum going phut, there a chestnut or a may tree kicking the bucket and then getting sawn up for our use by delightful old Mr Bidder from the village, aged 81 and a fine physical example to all apart from a troublesome bunion.

However, there is, in addition to the need to remove ash, restock the log basket and, in the morning, get the fires going, one disadvantage attached to open fires that may not be immediately apparent to everybody. We have, in addition to large lumps of wood, an abundance of shed-stored twigs (something that I am sure Mary Webb refers to as 'a tass of dry kindling'), but to get the twigs going, newspapers are required. 'Myrtlebank' indulges itself in those two very reputable sheets that aren't the *Guardian*, with the result that when I wish to refer to a paper of, say, three days ago, it is usually to find that it is no more, having that very morning gone up usefully in smoke and with a blazing fire to show for it.

And thus it comes about that I have unfortunately been unable to check something really rather weird that I read a few days ago, namely an announcement on that page that lists the movements and general activities of the nobs, together with cheering details of government hospitality – an announcement to the effect that Mr and Mrs Thatcher had thrown a party at No. 10 for 'some entrepreneurs'. The word was so bizarre and unusual and, indeed, so vague and unreal and deeply unsatisfactory, that it stuck in my mind (if I merely dreamt it, I apologise, though I tend not to dream of Downing Street, just reading about it by day being quite sufficient for my needs). Was it 'a group' of 'entrepreneurs'? Possibly, the word 'group' implying some sort of chummy cohesion. But no details were given: no numbers, no nationalities, no names, no menu, no nothing. And why on earth the French word 'entrepreneur'? We know that it means 'one who undertakes' but mockers must instantly abandon the idea that they were a team of undertakers. One presumed that, in the plural, they were businessmen or contractors or go-betweens, or something.

And then suddenly the truth dawned on me. Our gallant PM was soon to set off for Paris to bargain and attempt to reason with those rascally frogs about our outrageous EEC contributions and, ever conscientious and 'with it', was steeping herself and those about her in a French ambience prior to crossing the Channel (our channel, whatever they may say). What could be wiser? Knowing her, I bet she went full out and who can doubt that in the snug confines of her private quarters, she and what some popular papers refer to as Husband Denis dusted off and brushed up their French conversation in readiness, with cries at breakfast of *'Passez-moi, chéri, la Tip-tree's marmalade'* and, later in the day, *'Sapristi, que je suis fatiguée!'* and *'Ah, mes pauvres vieux pieds!'* What is the opposite, so to speak, of 'to anglicise'? Anyhow, did she do whatever it is with Mr Thatcher's Christian name and give it a frog sound? If you yourself are in doubt (one gets so rusty), let me help you. Say it DUR-KNEE. Thus, her sentences may have begun happily with *'Dis-moi, Dur-Knee'* and, at about 10 a.m. and as ministers start to arrive and car doors slam in Downing Street, *'Ecoute, Dur-Knee, voici le cabinet qui arrive.'* I am not too sure what the French equivalent of 'cabinet' is, and kind though you are, please don't write to tell me as I can safely struggle through to the end of Life's Pathway without garnering this little gem of knowledge. *Cabinet* has, as we know, another and far more useful meaning (*'Un moment, Dur-Knee, je dois aller au cabinet'*).

Which raises the whole question of Mrs Thatcher's French language abilities. If she has, as I suspect, merely a very reputable O Level, after which she hurried on, and why not, to Natural Sciences, then she was mad not to have conducted the whole of her conversations and discussions and interviews in France firmly in French (*'Non, non! Français seulement, j'insiste!'*) The French have always had a deep suspicion and distrust of anybody who speaks their language at all well but, pitiless though they are by nature, one has found in them a sort of amused benevolence towards those haltingly saying *'Où se trouve le Louvre?'* But as it was, what did we see relayed from the French television but a very English lady boldly confronting foreigners and self-confidently providing a fatal and unstoppable flow of English, hateful from the start to European ears and with a ring to it of a gym mistress haranguing an unsatisfactory class. She also made use, and could foolishness go further, of what I think must be rough boxing terms ('We shall go on fighting our corner', she kept saying, a phrase totally baffling to anybody unfamiliar with the world of fisticuffs). This was no way to get results and represented a sad misreading of the French character. And she recklessly reminded everybody of the existence, terminated though it may now be, of General de Gaulle – a disastrous name to bring out in the circumstances.

But with everything conducted in schoolgirl French, what a

difference there might have been! To start with, little whimpers of *'Pardon?'* and *'Parlez plus lentement, s'il vous plaît'*. Then simple little direct statements, such as *'Nous n'avons pas beaucoup d'argent'* and *'L'Angleterre est très 'hard up' et 'stoney-broke', comme nous disons familièrement'*. Then, in the frog torrent that would doubtless follow, there could have been little moaning interjections of *'Pas possible'* and *'Ciel!'* and *'Ca ne va pas'*. She could have fluttered a wispy little lace handkerchief, always such a powerful weapon in a female armoury, and dabbed an eye from time to time, with tiny mutterings of *'Je ne suis qu'une femme'*. Perhaps a loud and sudden shriek of *'Au secours!'* would have been going too far, and I rather fancy that those words are the exclusive property of people drowning and are specially reserved for them (*'Attention! Je descends pour la troisième fois!'*). At all events, there was an opportunity here, and one at which a Siddons would have clutched, for some fine dramatic acting. Any woman worth her salt can pretend to swoon and call for water – *'De l'eau!'* – and Mrs Thatcher didn't even do that. The whole thing was sadly muffed. And to those who object that acting plays no part in politics, my answer is 'Really?' Or, if you prefer it, *'vraiment?'*

# *Through the nose*

When people point out to me, as they sometimes do, that such and such a thing is 'within sight and sound' of something or other, they find me all alert attention, with eyes keenly focussed and ears cocked, for reasonably good eyesight and hearing are still, and how grateful one is, mine. But if, on the other hand, they were to say that this or that is 'within sight and smell' of whatever it is, they would find me the picture of dejection, not a bounce in me and all keenness vanished, for my sense of smell, once envied by dogs, has long since become enfeebled and has now almost completely atrophied. There are said to be male butterflies which can detect the exciting presence of a potential Mrs (or Madam) Butterfly at a distance of three miles. Not I. If I were a butterfly, celibacy would have to be my lot. Whatever lady butterflies use as their own personal Chanel No. 5, would never reach me, sniff and snuff the air as I may. It is no hardship really as I doubt if I could ever learn to love caterpillars. And I am not all that keen on cabbages.

It is indeed a moot point as to whether the inability to smell (and here I am obviously using the verb 'smell' in its transitive and more fragrant sense) is one of Life's pluses or minuses. Do feel free to consider the matter for yourselves and form discussion groups, making your very own lists of favourite smells and otherwise. Here, for such is the sunniness of my nature, I shall be concentrating mainly on the pleasant ones. As a boy, one of the sharpest pleasures on the first day of the hols was to wake up, in one's own good time and deafened by no clanging bell, in one's own little bed at home and without any boisterous schoolboy neighbours in other beds ('Oh do shut up and go and boil your head, Bellamy!'), and to become aware, and rising from the kitchen regions below, of the smell of bacon and eggs cooking, with an occasional intermingling, and heralded by piercing shouts of dismay, of burnt toast, not in itself at all disagreeable to the nose and swiftly put to rights by that vigorous scraping with a knife that, however large or small the piece of toast, covered the whole sink in a fine black mantle. Coupled with these was that of coffee being prepared for the adults, for one preferred in those days tea, and wafting in too from the landing came the warm smells of soap and hot water and towels as by then my father had had his bath and was arraying himself for the 8.42 a.m. to London. Quite an anxious little moment for the household whose duty it was to ensure that the breadwinner departed in jocund mood.

If my Essex grandmother happened to be staying with us, she brought with her, and all the way from Colchester, her own distinctive smell. She was a lovely, round, cosy and roly-poly lady whom I greatly loved and, on meeting her each morning at breakfast, one was warmly embraced. This had its perils for her front part seemed to be festooned with a mass of necklaces and brooches and beads and metallic objects (pince-nez on a chain) and if you didn't look out you got a section of her hearing-aid stuck rather painfully up your nose. Here the smell was entirely the very agreeable one of lavender for she belonged to the days when many ladies filled their drawers (and here I am referring specially to chests of drawers and tallboys and other wooden containers) with lavender bags, and spent part of their time making and embroidering lavender bags and then going out to what were called Sales of Work and buying lavender bags constructed and embroidered by other ladies. In this way they each amassed the fifty or sixty lavender bags without which life would have been considered intolerable. The other item always available at Sales of Work was the now vanished pincushion, pincushions in all sizes and shapes (sometimes they were like a heart) and colours, but pincushions do not, unless some misfortune has happened to them and they have been spilt on, smell and therefore play no part in our survey.

My mother was a splendid gardener, her cries of 'I'm just off to dead-head the border' mystifying and agitating non-gardening visitors who seemed to assume from her words that we had paying guests whom my mother, an unlikely figure with an axe, periodically beheaded. She had designed and made, with professional help for 'the heavy', her own Berkshire garden from a lush and gently sloping field which had for countless years been occupied by nothing but cows, the soil greatly benefitting from what the cows had, from time to time, left behind. As a result, everything flourished and, going out into the garden after breakfast (I was too old for 'May I get down now, please?' but still young enough to have to wait for a dismissive nod), one was welcomed by every sort of flower smell – roses, great clumps of pinks, lilies, honeysuckle and so on. We none of us greatly cared for those old-fashioned summer-houses, damp and thatched abodes of all kinds of crawling creature and often standing among gloomy laurels, and instead we had a flagged and roofed-in area where it was possible to sit comfortably in the shade, view the landscape o'er, sniff the whiffs, open the *Morning Post* (another pleasant smell) and read what the critic had to say about *Sunny* at the London Hippodrome (1926, if you're rusty), with Binnie Hale and Jack Buchanan and to a matinée of which one had been invited the very next week. I am well aware that this was an idle and privileged pre-war existence but I see no reason for being repentant about it. It was lovely while it lasted, and I shall keep saying so from the tumbril, as it rattles its way to the block.

School smells were, however, rather a different kettle of fish and the breakfast haddock being prepared in the house kitchen and in clouds of stream carried its fishy message upwards to the dormitories and alerted us to the fact that any moment now the bell would go and that breakfast was going to consist, and yet again, of haddock. The haddock was not alone in scenting the dormitory air. I do not wish to disgust or depress readers as sensitive as myself, who am the first to wince at Life's nastier sides, but, all the same, facts are facts and in those days there was, by morning and beneath each bed, a generously filled *pot de chambre*, a necessary (for the few lavatories were far away) but highly unhygienic receptacle which has long since disappeared together with the maids whose doubtfully pleasing task it was to empty them into fearful things called slop pails. And while we are in this sobering line of country, there was, in the village in which stood my prep school, Stirling Court on the Hampshire coast, a regular happening of an extremely displeasing nature. I do not know of what the local drains consisted, or if the sewage was collected in underground caverns measureless to man, but I do know that in the 1920s a sewage cart would arrive every so often and, letting down a large pipe through a man-hole, would pump up what lay all too obviously beneath. On our way to the playing-field, we frequently viewed and smelt, to cries of 'Pooh!' and '*Quel stink!*', the unlovely operation in progress. And in addition, the district, rich in farm land, was dotted with silos which also had their whiffy word to say, and our crocodile walks often saw the entire procession with rather grubby handkerchiefs pressed firmly to their noses.

At Stirling Court, damp smells predominated. Damp linoleum, swabbed with a mop, greeted one on emerging from a classroom. All our towels were in a permanent state of dampness and our games clothes, thrust into an airless locker and emerging as soggy as they went in, didn't have a chance. Pegs in a dank corridor supported our macintoshes and over-coats, always damp from the wet sea-air in which they had their outings. The table-cloths were damp (and it was a 1d fine if you spilt a tumbler and increased their dampness) and the food itself, particularly stews and cabbage, was watery. Watery too were the eyes of the headmaster, to whom we were much attached, but the eyes owed themselves less to water than to Scotch, though at the time we were too innocent to realise it and loyally attributed his rolling gait to a life on the ocean wave and the fact that Portsmouth and the Royal Navy were just around the corner and exerting their influence.

But taking it all round, and remembering the delicious smells from freshly macadamised roads, bread shops, lilac, pine bath essence, starched linen, tweed, woods after rain and Fortnum's Food Halls in all their succulent glory, I think I miss more than I gain. Is there such a thing as a smelling-aid?

# Dear diary

Embowered as one currently is in bougainvillaea (I write while on holiday) on the terrace of a charming clifftop hotel, with the Mediterranean (much cleaner than previously) sparkling below and the town of Amalfi a picturesque sight a mile away, it would be easy to abandon oneself completely (and I here use the verb 'abandon' in no loose or licentious sense) to this world where the Italian *dolce far niente* has full play and where one is tempted to think of nobody but oneself, and even that not very often. The only thing that is said to have worried Rudolph Valentino during his Hollywood career was not the hordes of screaming admirers but where the next plate of spaghetti was coming from. He should have remained in southern Italy. Here that is the least of our anxieties. Spaghetti comes and at regular intervals, piled high, scattered with parmesan and washed down with wine. It is followed, you can bet your bottom lira, by veal. Veal gives way to cheese and fruit, and our little meal is rounded with a sleep.

And thus it might go on day after happy day but for nagging thoughts of home. Far away as one is, one worries about loved ones left behind. How, for example, is dear Mrs Thatcher and has she planned a proper holiday for herself and Denis (I had a weird dream that they had rented a cafe at Sidmouth and, with Princess Anne dressed as a Nippy, were 'doing' Devonshire Teas at five bob a time). Well then, on which yacht and sailing whither will Mr Heath's jaunty cap be seen, that fine nose snuffing the breeze and our ex-Sailor PM ready to leap to the tiller and, in a Force 7 sou'wester, put her hard over, a phrase whose meaning and purpose have never been clear to me and which I have not cared to ask about as the words bear a hint of indelicacy.

As for Lord Carrington, there is a thoroughly odd and

persistent rumour along the coast here that he has, gig-lamps excitedly gleaming, rented a section of a famed Positano hotel just ten miles from here and that later in the year and during the state visit, the Royal Yacht is to put in (quite a feat of seamanship at that pierless town) and decant Her Majesty for, of all improbable things, cocktails. Apart from wondering what an Italian cocktail can taste like, can this venture possibly be true? Who is to be bidden to join them at the cocktail hour? In what lingo will the conversation be ('Permit me to replenish your sidecar')? Has HM any Italian more advanced than 'Kindly pass the ravioli'? and whither then would the Royal Yacht be bound? The pleasures of Capri and the Bay of Naples are greatly over-rated but the island of Ischia has much to offer. It surely cannot be true that the royal European *Wanderlust*, so strong and fully indulged in both Queen Victoria and Edward VII has, descending in the direct line, completely fizzled out. The main part of the royal festivities will of course occur in Rome and here I had another strange dream, namely that the Italians, hunting about for all that is brightest and best in the world of fireworks, would come upon a massive set piece in some dusty store house and, setting it off at the appointed time, would see before them, spluttering and fizzing away and lighting up the darkness, a giant face emerging – none other than Mussolini Triumphant.

Every so often we manage to get an English newspaper, two days late though the news it contains may be, and it cheers the heart to read once more of the joyous things of home – trains cancelled on the southern line, burglary figures up, ten mile tail-backs on the M5, and car sales plummeting. But there has been at least one English newspaper item that, shouted thrillingly from table to table in the restaurant, was received on all sides by us expatriates with the very heartiest of British cheers. Faces that have for days borne an anxious look, relaxed. Smiles replaced frowns. I refer, of course, to the Tate Gallery's lavish and generous outlay of £18,000 (money belonging to you and me really, I suppose, but let that pass) in order to secure at auction and at Sotheby's various 'Bloomsbury papers' for the nation and thus to retain in this country every scrap, whiff, shred and vestige of Woolfiana and associated names. The papers include 500 letters between Roger Fry and Vanessa Bell, at that time the object (or do I mean subject?) of Fry's devotion and of his stamps. Hooray for them, and hooray for us. Small wonder that our loud huzzas rang out. The papers are safe! Oh, the relief of it!

As interest in Bloomsbury and its inhabitants appears to increase yearly, except among those soulless few who have long since announced a feeling of surfeit, some coarsely even going so far as to say that they are fed up to the back teeth and beyond, I am wondering when the most favourable moment would be for me to release at public auction an interesting

*and he reports presence of a Mr L. Strachey*

possession that came into my hands a few years ago and which relates to the less aesthetic sides of these renowned persons. It is the diary of a Mr Alfred Maggs, proprietor of Messrs Maggs and Son, Sussex grocers and all-purpose purveyors and who, highly considered in their day, supplied the household needs of many families resident in a wide area of the county, among them the Bells at Charleston and the Woolfs at Monk's House, Rodmell. Charleston is, incidentally, although somewhat dilapidated, to be retained as a 'Bloomsbury monument' and, we hope, taken over by the National Trust with an endowment fund of £350,000. Oh hooray, again.

Mr Maggs, proud of his diary and of its literary associations, gave it towards the end of his life to another local resident, my Aunt Helen, herself prominent in the world of *belles lettres* (she was for many years 'Philomena' in the *East Sussex Clarion*), and she in her turn gave it to me, neither prominent nor in *belles lettres* but keen to do the best with it for myself and for the nation, in that order. 'Diary' is, perhaps, rather too grand a word for it as it merely consists of assorted jottings in a grocery order book, but 'Diary' is going to look a good bit better and more profitable in Sotheby's Catalogue than 'Assorted Jottings' and frankly, it is profitability that we are after.

A few excerpts will serve to give the tone of the book. 'April 9. Double order of potted meat and 1 lb of Best Back for Charleston can only mean Easter guests. Sent Sidney over on his bicycle and he reports presence of a Mr L. Strachey – "very chatty" and gave him a caramel'. 'May 4. The Woolfs busy stocking up for a visit from E. Smyth – Cooper's Oxford, Mazawattee tea, Bee-Zee-Bee honey and jars of calves foot jelly galore. Also several pots of Gentlemen's Relish (a great favourite with Dame Ethel, and Sidney in stitches over her hats)'. 'May 6. Crisis at Charleston. Mr Bell reported to have become "irregular" and not a grain of Bemax in the house. Sent Sidney over. L. Strachey gave him another caramel'. 'Sept 17. Mrs Woolf much put out that we do not stock Krackles ("The rusks that are kind to older tusks"). Sent over Chunklets instead but she sent them back with a rude note to the effect that Chunklets are not Krackles, a fact plain to all.' 'Aug 10th. Heat-wave brings mosquitoes and Roger Fry gets bitten in sensitive spot. Mrs Bell telephones urgently for tube of BUZZ-OFF Insect Repellent but have to tell her that I am grocer and not chemist, upon which she says something that sounds like a mixture of faugh! and tchah! and rings off.' 'Monk's House staff all on holiday and Mrs Woolf telephones and says "I am too busy to cook. What have you that is both edible and comes in tins?" Sent her over sardines, baked beans, pilchards and a jumbo pressed beef and hear no more.' 'Dec 23. Sidney had been hoping for his usual Christmas box (5/-) from the Woolfs but all he got was a signed copy of something called *The Waves*. Much disgusted.'

And so it goes on. A Robertson's 'Gollywog' strawberry for Charleston. The gas cooker explodes at Rodmell. The Charleston drains get blocked. Both households run out of lentils. As you see, underneath it all just ordinary people like you and me. I'm willing, of course, to sell the diary privately, provided it stays in England. Starting price: £10,000.

# Words, *words, words*

I place before you the humiliations that life showers on me as and when they occur. I keep nothing back. For a proper and mutual understanding it is essential that you should know the Whole Man, if I may so phrase it and myself. With me it is warts and all, though in my case the warts are much more likely to be carbuncles (and I here refer not to those fiery-red precious stones but painful and inflamed ulcers). Insulted by some, criticised by many, practically spat upon (and in quite good company, now that I come to think of it), I own up to everything, a markedly different approach to life now from that obtaining at my prep school in the 1920s where nobody ever dreamt of owning up who hadn't been actually detected in crime. So there we are then, you must take me or leave me, and preferably the latter, as you find me and my current humiliations are largely concerned with crosswords.

Every so often I take up the *Times* crossword and what do I see, and I am not here merely referring to this clue or that (6 across, 'clear the throat noisily for a bird of prey' in four letters. Answer: HAWK)? No. Before I even look at the clues, I see a statement at the top of the puzzle to the effect that this crossword was used in some competition or other and that 73 per cent of the competitors completed it correctly in 18 minutes, or some such sensational feat. I then start on the crossword, setting off my stopwatch at the same time, and after three hours on it (5 down, 'travel backwards for a stand-in' in three letters. Answer: SUB) I have achieved four answers, two of them a bit doubtful and but lightly pencilled in. Undeterred by constant failures of this description, and no Bruce's spider ever moistened its tentacles, or whatever it is they do, more pluckily than I before resolutely attempting the upward climb, I courageously tackled the other day *Times* Crossword No 15,252, adorned, I was relieved to see, with no boastful announcement concerning the success of others.

You probably remember well enough the crossword in question but just in case you don't, let me remind you that it was the one where the clue for 1 across, the answer to which was in two words, the first of eight letters and the second of five, was 'Reward for the brave warrior here'. Every crossword solver worth his salt knows perfectly well that the word 'brave' is a sort of trap and means not only brave but also a Red Indian, one of the old-fashioned ones and not a native of Bombay with socialist tendencies. The Red Indian that always springs to mind is, of course, Hiawatha. And what was his reward in life? None other than the lovely dusky Minnehaha with the black pigtails. And what was Minnehaha, a trying enough name in all conscience, also known as? Why, Laughing Water! And Laughing has eight letters and Water has five. So the answer to 1 across was, plainly, LAUGHING WATER and I wrote it boldly in.

The answer was, in point of fact, VICTORIA CROSS, nothing to do with Red Indians at all and a very feeble one, in my view, compared with the elaborate one that I had worked out. And if the answer was to be as stated, the clue is pretty feeble too and lamentably unimaginative. For 'Victoria Cross' a much more teasing clue would have been something like 'Monarch with the hump' and one could have pictured the solvers frantically trying to squeeze RICHARD THE THIRD into the space provided. To add insult to injury, a day or so later Minnehaha herself positively made an appearance among the clues, the last four letters of her extremely unfortunate name being used to indicate laughing and laughter. Rather cheap, I thought.

Finding myself the other day, surprisingly enough, in Wick (tippy topmost part of Scotland and a mere 14 miles from John o'Groat's), and finding there, equally surprising for such a relatively small town, a large and admirably stocked book-shop, I was wandering round it when my eye fell on the Collins 'Gem' Dictionary for crossword puzzles, 'a guide for success-ful puzzle-solving' and in a handy pocket size and selling at £1.20. Within, as I saw after I had hurriedly snapped it up, lie over 47,000 words listed under headings (Architecture, Sports, Art, etc) and, what is much more important, them-selves listed in alphabetical order and in sections *according to the number of letters the words contain*. Was there ever such ingenuity and thoughtfulness! Thus, stumped for the answer to 'fearsome fighting matter some fear' in five letters, you fly to the Warfare section and to the list of five-letter words and take your pick from over a hundred, among them blitz, Boche, foray, Gerry, H-bomb, kukri, Luger, sword, U-boat and uhlan (the preponderance of German words need surprise nobody with any sort of memory). The 'Gem' word selector is J. A. MacAuslane, to whom go both our warmest felicitations (13 letters) and congratulations (15).

A prominent feature of all crossword puzzles has always been the entirely seemly nature both of the clues and of the answers to them. Maiden aunts in droves can, and do, grapple with them without a blush. Bishops never need to hide them ('Ah, there you are, my dear') hurriedly under a cushion. Although the word 'knickers' is to be found in the 8-letter Clothing list, it is so embedded in such homely and similarly 8-letter things as galoshes, bedsocks, umbrella, surplice, polka dot, kiss curl and dove grey that the word causes no offence or suggests immodesty. However, I did have one moment of extreme anxiety (and here only Men of the World will be able to appreciate my misgivings). In the Clothing section, the words 'Dutch cap' appear and give one a bit of a start. But, sandwiched as they are between such confidence restoring things as dust-coat and ear-muffs, it is clear that the words can here only mean that charming feature of the national dress of Holland and a Dutch cap that is to be worn solely on the head.

As must have been only too clear over the years, I have a great fondness for jokes that aren't really very good ones and I am much attached to the old music-hall one which, usually uttered by a down-at-heel so-called stand-up comic, goes 'I have no money but my aunt has piles.' It was fired by the memory of this that I tackled the Medicine section of the 'Gem' booklet. How far, I asked myself, were the decorous firm of Messrs Collins prepared to go in the field of illness and cure? What, for instance, of 'piles' itself? Would it be allowed to appear? Hurrying to the 5-letter list, I hunted about for it. Not there! Belch, bowel, gripe, swoon and palsy are all there and ready for action but not a sign of piles, not even among the 12-letter list and tastefully camouflaged as haemorrhoids. Puke and that 4-letter wind noise are also banned. There is not even 'water' among the fives, let alone 'pass water' among the nines. But just in case you might be thinking that the Gem medical section takes an entirely narrow view of life, let me reassure you. Turn at once to the 10-letter section where you will find a joyous assembly of words, among them amputation, barium meal, Black Death, brain fever, broken nose, castration (rather going it, some might think), chloroform, convulsion, danger list, dipsomania, dizzy spell, drug addict, ear trumpet, Epsom salts, false teeth, flatulence (!) and knock-knees.

Being rather greedy, I take great pleasure in the Food and Drink chapter, right from the 3-letter words (bun, cod, eel, egg, pea, pig, roe, rum) through to the mouth-watering sounds of the 11s and 12s (marshmallow, pork sausage, profiterole, roast grouse, double cream, afternoon tea, codfish balls and the final splendour, smoked salmon). 'Scotch kisses' are also listed, whatever they may be or provide in the way of nourishment, the name striking a charmingly domestic and amatory note in the midst of so much good honest fare (scrambled egg, streaky bacon, whipped cream, pigs' knuckles and pickled onion).

# Full steam ahead

All admirers of Bulldog Drummond (and I do so like to picture him and poor old Phyllis, her perilous days of being gassed down the speaking-tubes of taxis long since over, in cosy geriatric retirement in the pseudo half-timberdom of somewhere like Sunningdale, yarning with pals over the wallop with Hugh now a bit wheezy perhaps and the jolly old muscles not quite what they were) will recall that, although no linguist, and there is very little evidence to show that either of the Drummonds ever read, or indeed even owned, a book of any kind, he was able on one thrilling occasion to summon up three words of Italian. Up in London and away from 'Myrtlebank' as I write, my literary base where the well-thumbed Sapper volumes are so constantly and eagerly referred to, I must speak from memory. It was in *The Black Gang*, I fancy, with Phyllis kidnapped and trussed up as usual and chained to a bed in devilish Carl Peterson's country hide-away, Maybrick Hall (the spirited girl had skilfully managed, even while being hijacked near the Ritz, to retain her parasol, important for the plot). Hugh, who has come through an electrified fence and is now creeping panther-like across to a dark Maybrick landing on the way to rescue her, bumps into a rascally Italian guard and before, as is Hugh's brisk way, knocking him out, he utters, perhaps to make the victim feel more at home, the only words from sunny Italy that he knows: *E pericoloso sporgersi*. It was *pericoloso* indeed for the guard. To guide her husband to her, Phyllis then manages, in some double-jointed way that Houdini himself would have envied, to rap on her bedroom door with the parasol – such an infinitely more ladylike protective appliance than an umbrella, with its Gamp associations. How clever Sapper was. Does she, when she sees Hugh, breathe 'My man!'? I expect so. She often did.

Now that so few English people travel anywhere in Europe

by train, the Italian words will be a novelty to many, for they do not for some reason put them on aeroplane windows, but older tourists will remember them well. Their counterpart in frog was *Ne pas se pencher au dehors* and both phrases were to be seen on compartment doors and they warned that it was wiser not to lean out of the windows, not so much for fear of getting smuts in the eyes but of having your nut bashed in as you passed some signal or water-tank or bridge or other solid and unresisting feature of the line. But because of the travel sickness that plagued me all though my childhood and youth, I was forced to ignore such warnings, either when abroad or at home, and became a deft hand at rattling down the window and depositing my breakfast or lunch outside. The upheavals almost always seemed to occur, particularly when going to London on the Great Western line of hallowed memory, when we were passing through a station (of which there were then many more), its up platform filled with commuters awaiting the slow train. I remember especially a row of startled and revolted and bowler-hatted faces at Slough as we glided past and I laid a rather liquid tribute at their feet.

But despite this minor gastric disability, I keenly enjoyed, and still do, rail travel. In memory's treasure-chest there sits an unusual outing as a boy from Oundle when, and I think it must have been in 1926, the entire school entrained and set off north west for the environs of Giggleswick in Yorkshire in order to observe the total eclipse of the sun, a treat denied to those living south or north of a certain cross-section of England. Our special train consisted of twelve restaurant carriages, one for each school house and the last one for the headmaster and assorted members of the staff. Seated at tables for four, we set off at dusk and before long a cold collation was served, what the frogs call with a sneer *assiette anglaise* and which consists of cold slices of beef and lamb and ham which have got left over from somewhere and which nobody can think what on earth to do with. There was then a substance called Mock Trifle (mock meaning no sherry) and, after a rather dashing boy called Duckworth had called for coffee and brandy and had been refused, we composed ourselves for slumber, not easily come by when seated at a table. One simply laid one's head down among the crumbs.

Whatever route can we have taken through the night? We certainly went first to Peterborough, but then where? Up to

*and I laid a rather liquid tribute at their feet*

Leeds, I assume, and then somehow along the Ribble valley. At all events, dawn found us, chilly and unwashed, detraining in a slightly rusty siding from where we were shepherded down a path and into a soggy field, clutching sections of smoked glass through which to gaze at this wonder of the heavens without being blinded. The chief science master informed us, through a megaphone, of the passing of time and the approach of the eclipse and urged us to note, among other things, the behaviour of the animal kingdom. The day was, alas, heavily overcast but it certainly grew steadily darker and the birds were clearly extremely puzzled. Near us, and less puzzled, was a largish cow who just stood languidly there, brooding quietly to herself. Although the diminishing sun was totally obscured by thick clouds, I do remember a rather strange eerie feel in the air, reported on to one's parents in the following Sunday letter

('There was this sort of eerie feel in the air'). Gradually it grew lighter again, the megaphone informed us that the excitement was now over, three cheers were given for the organisers of the outing (two rather jolly masters who blushed becomingly) and before long we were rumbling home and tucking into bacon and eggs, nourishment which I successfully deposited through the window and onto the platform at, I think it must have been, Doncaster. Still, all in all it had been a novel and pleasing trip and one had managed to miss both a Latin lesson and a Latin prep. What a remarkably enterprising and go-ahead school Oundle was and is. Stuffier establishments in the country had totally ignored the eclipse, had stayed right there where they were and had missed all the fun, cloudy though some of it had been.

I now greatly regret, when it is too late, never having travelled on the Orient Express, a splendid book by that name, written by E. H. Cockridge and published by Allen Lane at £5.95, now revealing all that one has missed. It seems to have been about 1860 that the idea of really *de luxe* rail travel took root and a lot of people got busy. Pullman (he came from Gregory Gulch, Colorado) panelled his coaches in walnut, supplied brass fittings and laid down deep-pile carpets, and President Ulysses S. Grant travelled on them and in them. In Europe the Wagons-Lits started up, the idea of actual sleep while awheel firing the imagination of another American, Colonel Mann, who delighted the public with his Boudoir Sleeping Car Company. And back in Europe again there was the Orient Express, its inaugural trip in 1883 being reported to goggling British readers by the obese and whiskery Paris correspondent of *The Times*, a flamboyant figure called Opper de Blowitz, with Opper marvelling at the silver cutlery, the waiters in powdered wigs and breeches, the ten course dinner, the speaking-tubes for summoning servants (*'Encore du champagne!'*), the marble fixtures, the club-like smoking-room, the *salon pour les dames* (ladies were advised to equip themselves with hatpins in case a gentleman should forget himself in a tunnel). As the train went further east, Opper was to be seen in a sort of Tyrolean rig – very wide knickerbockers, crumpled hiking jacket and a saucy and beplumed hat and was instantly taken for a Calabrian bandit (*'Non, non, moi je suis Opper de Blowitz'*).

Down the years the excitements have been terrific – derailments, ambush by brigands, hostages taken and ransoms demanded (the average German industrialist worked out at about £900 a head), the famous snow drifts which immobilised the train for a week, the glittering years when you could hardly move for Hapsburgs, spies and mistresses, and the merry moment in 1920 when the sixty-four year old French President tumbled out by mistake in his pyjamas (no bones broken but one slipper missing). You'll want to know what happened to Opper. He was finally awarded the Order of Medjidieh (Third Class) by Abdul the Damned. There now!

# Happy birthday

I do not much care for novelty (no power on earth is ever going
to get me onto a hang-glider or one of those surf-boards with a
sail and off which people fall into the sea) and for many years
now I have fought against the wide use at 'Myrtlebank' of
tea-bags. I am far from happy about their bogus and clinical
and synthetic white appearance before immersion (one bag for
you, and one bag for me, and none for the pot) or, after
immersion, their depressing and lukewarm brown sogginess
and the unacceptable feel of them before they find their way
into the trash-can (I have a contraption called a pedal-bin,
worked by pressure from the foot – to have been a bicyclist is a
help – and a household boon if ever there was one) and the lid
comes clattering down and removes them from sight. I have a
suspicion that tea tastes better if direct contact is made be-
tween boiling water and fragrant leaf, rather than filtered
through a sort of gauzy envelope that looks, before use, all too
like a small emergency dressing in a casualty ward ('Nurse
Rackstraw will attend to you – over here, Edyth').

I am also convinced, however much professional cooks may
disagree with me, that meat likes the proximity of a flame and
that joints cooked in a gas-oven have a richer taste than those
roasted by electricity, graciously though kind guests may greet
one's own efforts in this latter culinary field ('Your leg is a
dream of succulence'). How widely, one wonders, have fore-
igners, few of them tea-drinkers, taken to tea-bags? On my
recent holiday in Amalfi, we ordered, one hot and thirsty
afternoon, tea on the terrace and it arrived, complete with
tea-bags, labels hanging down from inside the tea-pot inform-
ing us that the name of this brand of tea-bag was SIR WINSTON
and, plainly, a British bag. It certainly provided restorative tea,
a liquid that was never, I would think, of very much interest to
that revered figure.

My Devon grandmother, also not one for novelty, would have much disapproved of tea-bags. Though not herself a geisha, her tea-making ceremonies would have easily outstripped, in elaboration and duration, anything that the inscrutable Japanese could dream up in one of those dainty tea-houses. Surrounded by tea-caddies (she favoured a blend of Earl Grey and finest Darjeeling, the latter to 'give it body'), a steaming kettle on a stand above a spirit-lamp, a sugar bowl and slices of lemon, a silver tea-pot, a milk jug and an array of rather pretty Rockingham tea-cups, she got busy, if her somewhat languid movements may be so described. Even when the tea was brewed and one was panting for a sip, each tea-cup had to be partially filled with hot water to warm it up, the water then being emptied into a, odious word, slop basin. My grand-mother invariably wore at tea-time one of those dresses with long and dangling sleeves and which, with the Rockingham at maximum risk, had to be held back with the other arm, thus reducing her general mobility and effectiveness, though contri-buting greatly, like those Japanese bows, to the stately nature of the proceeding. From the opening of the first caddy to the moment when she looked up and said, with a rising inflection, 'Tea, anybody?', twenty minutes had gone by – in childhood, a lifetime. And being the youngest present, one got one's tea, naturally, last, an arrangement as doubtfully just as that which obtained at school when they said, preparing to dispense something, 'Line up in alphabetical order' (hard cheese on the Zuckermans of this world but jolly for the Annans. One only hopes that being first in line at a youthful age does not carry with it any damaging psychological element).

The relationship between grandparents and grandchildren is often a highly pleasing one (all spoilings, and no naggings, the latter being the parents' happy privilege), but alas, I could establish no sort of acceptable rapport with my Devonian grandmother, for I looked at that age all too like my father, and between him and her the rapport had been negligible. She seemed incredibly ancient and wrinkled and wizened and I have sometimes wondered, while perhaps waiting for a bus (probably a No. 22, queen of the fleet), how old she was when I first, around 1914, became aware of her. And this very day and in the weird way that such things happen, I have been able, after all these years, to find out.

As most reviewers of literature know, one's tables and

window-seats are apt to pile up with attractive books kindly sent by publishers and authors, understandably anxious that their products should have as public an airing as possible and which indeed one does one's best to encourage and foster. It is no longer as easy as it once was to dispose, at half price, of unwanted review copies, and books come whizzing back with letters saying 'Thank you but we already have 89 copies of *Feast Not Thine Eyes* and can accept no more'. So space on shelves must be found for many of them and this involves a periodical thinning out of books (hospitals are, I find, glad of them and, priced at 5p, they go like hot cakes at church fêtes). However thoroughly one weeded last time, one can always find at least fifty more books that now qualify for the chop and thus, recently ferreting about, and reluctantly, among some novels of Charlotte M. Yonge (a prime favourite of my mother's) and deciding that *The Penniless Princesses* would have to go, I suddenly came upon my father's birthday book, chock-a-block with entries in my parents' handwriting, and there is my grandmother's name, with 'Born 1843' alongside. She was already 67 when I was born, and by non-rapport time was into the 70s. How odd that both in childhood and in youth, one hadn't even the very faintest idea of the age of anybody who wasn't also a child.

I cannot imagine where, all this time, *The Blue Birthday Book*, published in 1892, has been lurking. It provides, I see, 'proverbs, maxims and quotations for every day of the year', is of course of mainly a pious nature, and goes in strongly for rhyming couplets, such as 'Do not hurry, do not flurry: Nothing good is got by worry', with a sprinkling of Shakespeare and Longfellow and quite a lot that the editress, Mary Trebeck, seems to have manufactured under her own steam ('The devil will be where we think he's not: Security's Vale is his favourite spot'). Some of her advice is doubtful in the extreme, for example 'If you wish to be well, and you do I've no doubt, Just open the window before you go out' – a clear invitation to Burglar Bill to pop a leg over the sill, leave a message of contempt on the carpet and then hook it briskly with the plate.

It is far from difficult to get, on occasion, quite fairly ratty with Ms Trebeck. What about, for instance, 'He that would please all, and himself too, Undertakes much more than he can do', which would be a suitable house builder's motto ('We're hoping to get around to you again some time next month'). Then, those whose birthdays are on July 3rd are provided with the following piece of misinformation: 'Sands make the mountains high; Moments the years that fly; Trifles, life's history.' Mountains are very seldom composed of sand, and to inform, say, a Crimean veteran, who lost a leg at Inkerman and, on returning home, found that his wife had done a bolt with the butler, that his life's history has been composed of trifles, would qualify the authoress for a swipe to the head with his wooden leg. And what about those who, born on February 16th, look eagerly to the birthday book for a word of comfort – a *pensée* from Tennyson, perhaps, a few bracing words from Smollett or a heartening line from Bishop Wordsworth of Lincoln. What do they find instead? 'The sharper the blast, the shorter 'twill last' – just a rubbishy weather hint of very doubtful veracity and one which one would scarcely care to pass on to the luckless many who were in the devastating path of Hurricane Allen.

As to Ms Trebeck's sadly ineffective medical information ('Three doctors that can cure more than any other can, Dr Diet, Dr Quiet and Dr Merriman'), the less said the better, and although woefully little is known of her as a hostess (I seem to see her in furnished rooms at Worthing), there are grounds for thinking that her little 'dos' lacked vivacity and interest ('Him to my table I do not invite, Who loves by words an absent friend to bite'). And turning to my own birthday, May 10th, what idiocy do I find? 'One ploughs, another sows; Who will reap, no one knows?' Try telling *that* to the many splendid farmers whose fields lie in and around Appleton.

# *Boots boots boots boots*

Invited earlier in the year to appear, if this doesn't seem too much like boasting, on the Russell Harty TV show, lavishly brought to us in glorious colour (I come out predominately beetroot) by London Weekend TV, I was asked a question by this charming interviewer concerning my NS work and its possible message and, briskly throwing aside the frivolous mask and speaking in all seriousness and from the heart, I replied immodestly that I regarded myself as being the Jeanette MacDonald of the prose world. Alas, the unthinking chose to suppose that I was joking but this was far from being so. I did not by this imply an approaching sex-change into another and even naughtier *Naughty Marietta*. I merely meant that, like that toothy songster from the world of celluloid, I too provide harmless, humdrum and airy nothings at regular intervals. I myself, as you'll have long since discovered to your advantage, can easily be ignored and avoided whereas, in her heyday, it was virtually impossible to avoid Miss MacDonald. But then, who wanted to?

Having followed attentively, as I always did, her dazzling career, there is one question to which I have never found a completely satisfactory answer. I mull the problem over from time to time and yet the puzzle remains a puzzle, its solution for ever maddeningly hidden. To get at the truth, one would need to have all her films shown simultaneously in some vast arena, a musical treat probably too difficult to arrange. The unanswerable query is, in which of her many films did Miss MacDonald actually sing *loudest*? She was certainly at full voice in both *The Vagabond King* and *Rose Marie*. Sometimes I think that *One Hour With You* was loudest, sometimes *The Merry Widow*. Ah well. Never mind. She provided, in *The Love Parade*, one of my favourite moments in films. She was, I think, a Princess of some foreign kind and, abandoning for the moment her dream lover, Maurice Chevalier, she strode forth, dressed as a Grenadier, to review her troops. They sang, and she, heaven knows, sang right back at them. At one point, facing them all drawn up on parade, she shrieked, with no trace of emotion, the line 'My heart is aflame with your loyalty'. Delicious.

How different and exciting prewar life would have been for the boys in the Oundle School OTC if we had had tuneful Miss MacDonald to review us. The OTC was periodically 'inspected' but only by Major-Generals with gingery moustaches. The initials OTC stood, of course, for Officers' Training Corps, though I could never quite follow whether this meant that we were all being trained to be officers or were merely a batch of cannon-fodder being marched about by officers to keep *them* in training. As the phrase 'officers and gentlemen' was then popular, I rather fancy that the former of the two explanations is the correct one, much emphasis being laid in our scholastic life on gentlemanly behaviour. To remain in the ranks would then have been far from gentlemanly. The OTC has been renamed the CCF, which stands for Combined Cadet Force and is much more realistic. I gather that participation in it is nowadays a good bit more enlivening than in my day, when nothing remotely interesting ever happened and total boredom reigned supreme. Our hearts were aflame with nothing whatsoever except resentment. Nobody could have appeared less like dear Jeanette than the officers who commanded us. Deepest depression was their, and indeed our, portion.

But I seldom remained depressed for very long. As with some other occupations in school life, we learnt to remove the mind by inventing a dream world to which we could fly and there was to hand a meaty antidote to the OTC in the shape of the enormously popular Foreign Legion yarns of P. C. (Percival Christopher) Wren. When marching endlessly down the dusty, winding roads of Northamptonshire (in other circumstances, a county of great charm and beauty), it helped greatly to imagine that we were in North Africa and about to be attacked at any moment by rascally Arabs and Touaregs whose age-old customs, after a skirmish, of laying out and paying the last courtesies to their enemy dead left so very much to be desired, not to speak of one or two portions missing. On field days against other schools, our battle cry of 'death to the infidel!' much startled the saintly boys of the opposing forces (usually

*We were in North Africa and about to be attacked . . .*

Rugby or Uppingham). But I fear that none of our officers, in addition to failing to look like Jeanette MacDonald, could manage the faintest resemblance to the tyrannical Sergeant Lejaune (*jaune* my foot) of *Beau Geste* with his thrilling brutalities and insults and cross-patch cries of 'God smite you, you unspeakable corruption!' and 'I'll teach you, you swine!' and 'Silence, dog!'

But it is extraordinary to discover that, apart from the really wild improbabilities of Wren's masterpiece (words normally reserved solely for St Paul's but which are here intended for *Beau Geste*), the descriptions of life in the Legion appear to have been little exaggerated. Simon Murray, late of Bedford School, joined the Foreign Legion in 1960 during the North African upheavals, and his book, *Legionnaire* (Sidgwick & Jackson, £6.95) tells of his five years' service in the breezy manner of a public school prefect showing off a little in the common room. Rigged out in the uniform with the blue cummerbund and bright red epaulettes (which we last saw, I fancy, on Gary Cooper), he knows what to do when some skulking Spaniard pinches his seat on the train ('I yanked him to his feet and threw him the length of the carriage'). Foreigners aren't too greatly admired, especially a swarthy frog ('He's puke-making and has guts made of lime juice') and Lieutenant Lasalle ('little French creep') and Lieutenant Otard ('rather wet-looking'), but how very jolly that it's hooray for us all over everywhere ('The English appear to be held in high regard'). And so, with an occasional home-sick thought ('Oh to be in England – parties, friends, *The Times*'), a musing or two about Life ('How quickly turns the wheel of fate') and grapes in abundance ('one hell of a laxative'), he settles down to the extremely Spartan regime interspersed with the comforts provided by stupendous boozing and, in Mr Murray's case, enormous food parcels arriving at intervals from Fortnum and Mason.

By way of keeping order, the NCOs laid about them with rifle butts ('Ledermann is down to his last three teeth') but the right sort of chap can always admire here and there 'a certain toughness, indelible in those who are made of the right fibre'. I regret to say, however, that there are some wonky fibres about and that there were 136 deserters in the space of four months. Chaps from comprehensives, I wouldn't be at all surprised.

# I've got a little list

Regular readers, already familiar in their minds' eyes with the general layout of the spacious grounds in which stands stately 'Myrtlebank', with all of its main windows facing due south and with the terrace, resplendent with potted geraniums in assorted colours, forming what some like to call a sun-trap, may care for a supplementary word or two about the orchard in a corner of which this outstandingly pleasing residence is situated. The orchard is on a slope that gently rises towards the west and extends to roughly three acres as far as my eye can tell, though some eyes consider it to be four, and it is intersected by a charming stream that comes from haunts of coot and hern and makes a sudden sally, and sparkles out among the fern to bicker down our valley and I sometimes think that an agreeable poem might be written about it in the style of, say, Tennyson, with a thoughtful line or two to the effect that men may come and men may go but brooks go on for ever, thus putting us firmly in our places with a sobering reminder of the relatively ephemeral nature of mankind (or do I now have to say personkind?) when compared with brooks and streams.

Before I move on, by one of those natural transitions for which this column is so justly noted, to a splendid literary treat that was sent to me and is now available to all, let me just say a word about a currently popular subject, namely brand of apple, for my orchard, being an apple orchard, contains apples. I know that you will, in your friendly way, rejoice to learn that this year's harvest can only be described as bumper. It was originally entirely a cider-apple orchard and one of about four hundred trees, but age and decay and storms have, down the years, removed half of them and we have assiduously planted in their place eaters and cookers and now, evenly balanced, are enjoying the results, with the heavily-laden boughs sweeping the ground.

Picking (an exciting moment) has begun, our Beauty of Bath

being, as always and like an elder daughter, the first to go. We have no truck whatsoever with that apple with which the fraudulent frogs plan to flood this country (how dare they, and on top of that lamb business too?), nor shall we here take the slightest notice of those officious busybodies who appear to be telling us what apples we may grow for the future. Our various varieties can but remain, in these parts, prime favourites. What more noble cooking apple exists than Lord Derby, or one that remains firmer than Bramley's Seedling? Housewives requiring an apple that fluffs up a little in the pot can hardly do better than Lane's Prince Albert or Monarch. For a dessert apple, what about Laxton's Superb or Ellison's Orange, with James Grieve as a standby? I look, and I look with confidence, to Mrs Thatcher to halt the unacceptable flow of Golden Delicious, show the French yet again what's what ('*Ecoute, Giscard . . .*') and, though perhaps it is too much to hope for, remove us entirely and at once from the dreaded EEC, a disastrous body as far as we are concerned and one to which I have been from the start opposed. Whoever in their senses would imagine any good coming to *us*? That old General must be splitting his sides.

But now for the treat. Did you chance to notice a recent snap in a popular daily of our PM, dear Mrs T, neatly attired as is her wont and bandbox-fresh and getting stung on the nose by a wasp? That, I hasten to say, is not the treat and the little incident occurred while she was, as ever regardless of self, inspecting a Cambridge factory and saying a cheery word of encouragement all round. And did you at the same time chance to wonder how many ministers of state in the world's history had been bitten by wasps or been savaged by wolves or gobbled up by tigers and if there was anywhere a list of such persons? The likelihood is, believe it or not, that somewhere such a list exists, for a mind-boggling volume called *The Book of Lists 2* (the first *Book of Lists* appeared in 1977), published by Elm Tree Books at £5.95, has come my way, full of lists sent in by listomaniacs and compiled by a team of four. A few of the titles will give you the general spirit of the thing – 18 Men or Women Who Slept With 3 or More Celebrities, 6 Incestuous Couples of the Bible, The 8 Most Awful Warships in History, 8 Generals Who Never Won a Battle, 10 Well-Known People Who Died in Someone's Arms, and 7 Persons Who Have Gone Over Niagara Falls in Barrels.

One has, naturally, one's favourites. 12 Great Slips of the Tongue in American Politics reveals Ronald Reagan, speaking in 1975 about the third-world countries, saying 'The United States has much to offer the third world war', and saying it, what is more, nine times: and at the height (or do I mean depths?) of the Watergate scandal, Richard Nixon was heard to say 'This is a discredited president' (it is assumed that he meant to say precedent). Then, for a British person, the 10 Most Defeated Nations in Modern History makes delightfully stimulating reading, with Turkey prominently placed at the head of the list and with France doing fine work at No. 5. 12 Possible Sites For The Garden of Eden includes the east bank of the Mississippi river near the Minnesota border, while Noah was later resident, until the Flood carried him east, at Gales-ville, Wisconsin. 16 Notable Persons Struck by Lightning has a retired park ranger in Virginia who, between 1942 and 1977, was struck seven times, losing his eyebrows and a big toenail. I do not wish to go into the indelicacies of Double-Sexed Animals: suffice it to say that there are 14 of them, and nor do I intend to give details of 21 Famous Women Who Breast-Fed Their Babies apart from asking what is so special about that.

I am glad to report that, while there are 12 Famous Cat Lovers, there are only 10 Famous Cat Haters, among them Shelley, Ronsard, Bonaparte, Boswell, Eisenhower and Brahms, who tried to pick off neighbours' pussies with a bow and arrow while he should have been thumping the Bechstein. Particularly impressive, and splendidly cheering for the schol-astically idle, is the list of 15 Celebrated Persons Who Got Miserable School Reports – Wellington, Zola, Heine, Picasso, James Watt, Puccini, Chesterton, Churchill, Henry Ford and, you'll hardly believe it, Darwin, Edison and Einstein, while the list of those expelled from school or 'asked to leave' includes John Barrymore (discovered celebrating Washington's Birth-day in a brothel), Orville Wright ('mischievous behaviour'), Trotsky (ragging teacher), Bogart ('Irreverence'), Mussolini (throwing an inkpot at teacher) and Dali (sulking at art teacher's jibes).

Do please spare a thought for 10 Eminent Constipation Sufferers – Robespierre, even while the guillotine clanged down, was a martyr to it, ditto Bonaparte (said to munch too fast. What a lesson!). Freud's spastic colon brought constipa-tion, and the reverse, with it, while Gershwin put his sluggishness down to 'composer's stomach'. Howard Hughes and poor Judy Garland must also be added, together with a costive Henry James (a snap of him strolling on the beach at Rye in 1907 looks as though it was taken during an exceptionally distressing bout). Well then, did you realise that there are 5 Body Parts Named After Italians and all of them fairly useful – Organ of Corti (internal ear), Eustachian Tube, Fallopian Tubes (Ladies Only), Ruffini's Corpuscles and Sartoli Cells (Gentlemen Only and in an area best left unmentioned).

From now on, my dinner table conversation is going to fascinate one and all. 'Did you know that in 1975 a Detroit baby fell 14 storeys and landed on a man called Joseph Figlock (baby unharmed) who happened to be walking below, and exactly a year later another baby descended on Joseph Figlock, who began to think twice before taking a breather?' 'Did you know that an Iowa cow called Fawn was, in 1962, swept up by a tornado and alighted safely after a maiden flight of half a mile, and in 1967 she took off again, reaching a goodly altitude and again landing undamaged, this time near a bull?'

Readers of the book are encouraged to make their own interesting lists and send them (not, for pity's sake, to me) to a given address. 'Don't be listless' coax the compilers, funsters all.

# Painted lady

In the dear, dead and happy days before the world at large became so skilful at seeing through and denigrating everybody and everything and when one was encouraged to look up to people rather than down one's nose at them, we all at my prep school, Stirling Court, had an immense admiration for an Australian cricketer called W. H. Ponsford. He would have been at that time in his mid-twenties and snaps showed a charming, healthy, square-cut face, not unlike one of those delightful Bedsers. Why we should have lighted on him, who can say, but light we did. In our pencil and paper games of what was called dab cricket, he went in first, as indeed he did in life, with W. M. Woodfull and, by dint of half-opening one's eyes before bringing the pencil down by mistake on a 'Run Out' or 'Caught Long-on', one was able to make him score century after century (he once made 429 against Tasmania but, much as we revered him, it would have taken too long, impatient as we were for a win, to make him notch up 429).

At least two daily papers, and three Sundays, supply an eager public with details of birthdays, culled no doubt from *Who's Who*, sometimes of well-known public figures still flamboyantly before us, and sometimes of unknowns who, as far as one is concerned, have been modestly labouring in secret and hiding their lights under bushels (Lady Jean Sidebotham, 78. J. de B. Pincock, 94. The Hoot of McHoot, 103) and it was with some emotion that I saw in my *Daily Telegraph* that on Sunday, October 19th, W. H. Ponsford would be 80. He lives still, and hooray for that, and one's mind flies instantly to others of one's youthful heroes and heroines. Jack Buchanan is, very sadly, dead and those lazy, lissome limbs (so much more restful than Astaire's) delight no more, but Binnie Hale and Dorothy Dickson are with us yet and long may it be so. The lady whom many consider to have been the world's best golfer of either sex, Joyce Wethered, kindly and contentedly shows endless visitors round her beautiful and famous gardens at Knightshayes outside Tiverton. What, I wonder, of dear Betty Nuthall, so like, in many ways, our admirable Christine Truman, both of them so very very nearly so very very good? A happy grandmother, perhaps, occasionally coaxed on court ('Now, you're not to make granny run!') for a knock-up with grandchildren? I do hope so, for she belongs to a time when there were charming, smiling faces to be seen at Wimbledon, now rather a rarity.

Among the people deeply admired by my father (Stanley Baldwin, Dickens, Joseph Paxton, Scott of the Antarctic) there was a spinster lady whose life and *raison d'être* were both wrapped in complete mystery but, whenever the conversation at home chanced to turn to the Pankhursts, or Grace Darling, or Nurse Cavell or any other staunch woman with noble and brave deeds to her credit, my father seldom failed to wind up the proceedings, so to speak, by saying 'Ah, but just look at Miss Cattermole!' We looked indeed, but we looked in vain. We had her name, but what her fame? What had placed her, not only in the intrepid class, but also at the top of the ladder? It never quite did to ask my father a direct question, for the answer, if such it may be called, was likely to be 'And why do you ask?', which somewhat interrupted the free and friendly flow of chat. If one had said, factually but rudely, 'Because I want to know', huffy looks and moody silences would have followed. My mother, cross-questioned as to Miss Cattermole's obviously sensational achievements, said 'Oh, she's that woman of your father's who did something helpful for strikers at a factory gate' and then, seeing that she had implied that Miss Cattermole had 'obliged' a line of unemployed, she burst, as usual, into loud shrieks and we had, as so often with us, to discontinue the conversation in case total hysteria set in. So, unfortunately, I learnt no more and my father died with the answer to the Cattermole Riddle in his eternal keeping.

How greatly he would have relished, for she stands almost alone in the field of really sustained female intrepidity, Miss Margaret Fountaine, a Victorian lady who travelled the world netting butterflies and men in almost equal quantities and it is not always easy to tell which catch the affectionate diurnal lepidopterist prized more though, despite a lot of – revolting phrase – 'heavy petting', her imperilled virginity didn't actually go pop until she was 41 (she was given to yelling 'Hook it!' to over-intense suitors and she had at command a fine string of oaths). In 1940 this unusual woman was discovered dying by a road-side in Trinidad, her butterfly net at hand and still, at 78, on the hunt, at least for butterflies. She had prudently arranged for her diaries, which run to well over a million words, her sketch books and her ten enormous display cases containing 22,000 butterflies, to be deposited (not to be touched until 1978) with the Castle Museum in Norwich and now, expertly and wittily edited by W. F. Cater, Miss Fountaine's revelations burst upon us in *Love Among the Butterflies*, published (and a real snip at £8.50) by Messrs Collins, with enchanting colour plates and innumerable gorgeous butterflies.

In the last century it was never easy for a spinster to escape from home but she achieved this welcome feat in 1891 when, aged 29 and with a small private income, she set off quite alone for Geneva and, eventually, Naples, Corsica, Switzerland, France, Palestine, Egypt, West Indies, Bournemouth, South Africa and Australia. She was, as they say, between men. At Norwich there had been the curate, Mr Swindell and an Irish chorister, tipsy Septimus Hewson ('I felt him touch me as he looked under my umbrella') who sang 'Oh Rest in the Lord' so attractively prior to jilting her. A brisk reference to 'the raging fires of passion that rend my breast', a happy realisation that the world of Scarce Swallowtails and Camberwell Beauties is the one for her, and then, in Florence, up pops Signor Scafidi, who forgets himself ('Worthless buffoon'). In no time at all, and after an exciting sighting of a Greater Tortoiseshell ('I sprang up and seized my net'), Dr Galli-Valerio gets fidgety in Milan but is helpful with cough mixtures. A change of hair style and her smart 'butterfly attire' attracts three Palermo youths ('I found they belonged to the fastest set in town') who, as a ruse, ask to see her butterflies, a predicament from which a Baron rescues her (*'Vous êtes si jolie, si blanche'*) and, seeking a reward, has to be cooled off (*'Je ne fais pas ça'*). And here I have to say that Miss Fountaine was quite shameless in leading men on, though there is an uglier verb for it.

The diary was dotted with excellent studio portrait photographs, some reproduced here, of Miss Fountaine at various stages – aged 19, 26, 37 (with bicycle), 40 and 50. It is a firm, thin-lipped, long-nosed face, handsome rather than pretty, and one begins to wonder whether some of her amatory moments were possibly something of a figment of those raging and unstoked fires. Anyhow, on, between butterflies, they relentlessly went. There was a young Italian at Messina, aged only twenty-three ('I was twenty-six, ahem!' quips our girl, being a good old 34) and, on a visit home, a friendly lad from Wallace's Cycle Depot. In Hungary there was whiskery Dr Popovich who brought up her breakfast coffee and stole a kiss ('I overlooked the impertinence'). There were admiring glances at the Budapest Entomological Society meeting and, though in general she shows a preference for foreigners ('I suppose that Englishmen do make love sometimes, too'), in a crisis almost any man will do, be he an Egyptian ship's officer ('He told me I looked forty. Of course I instantly denied it'), a vice-consul, a coffee planter (keen on free love) or a Hungarian (*'Guten Abend'*) up to no good ('I jumped on my bicycle').

And then, after lecturing in Jamaica on The Sagacity of Caterpillars, true love arrived in the unexpected form of a married Syrian dragoman ('I love very much your legs') with whom she lived, in almost total happiness and partly in West Hampstead, for years. A splendid woman. What a shame that she existed before the days of 'This Is Your Life'.

# Tirra-lirra

In a weekly column such as mine, questions of tone and good taste are all important. In a regular offering of limpid prose prominently placed in the first half of a respectable magazine, nothing must shock, nothing must agitate, or all is lost. One word out of place and the reader starts to wonder what on earth he is in for next. It is for this reason that I have always set my face resolutely against anything that has about it even the faintest suggestion of being 'smut'. From the age of twelve on, I was warned, and almost daily, of the dangers of 'smut' and it is a warning which, as you see, I have heeded. No seed of advice ever fell or blossomed on richer soil. And therefore, when I pass on to you, as I am about to do, a risqué story, I do so merely in order to demonstrate what people can get up to who have not heeded 'smut' warnings and whose seeds have blossomed in quite other directions. And so, late in the day though it may be for such persons, this selfless disregarding of my principles is really intended as a further warning for the less fortunate.

This risqué story centres on Henley, whose river activities are at their apogee as I write. As the point of the story involves, as I said 'smut', I naturally do not understand it, but some of you may be able to work it out for yourselves or get it explained to you by somebody who was never warned about 'smut'. So, for better or worse, here goes. I gather that at Henley it is the custom among hearty rowing men who have just won a race to celebrate victory by throwing into the river the cox who has been steering their boat and loudly abusing them and bossing them about and urging them on to greater efforts and so on. A watery dip is by way of reducing him to size (usually rather small). An American visitor, seeing from a distance some boisterous horse-play going on, asked what was happening. 'Oh', was the reply, 'the crew are just putting their cox into the river. It's an old Henley custom'. The American looked very nonplussed and walked away muttering 'Ask a silly question, get a silly answer.' There you are. Make of it what you will. To the pure, all things are pure and I, of course, am totally baffled by the pleasantry and can hardly ask Canon Mountjoy, a man of the world if ever I saw one, for an explanation. Nor do I wish one. In this case, ignorance is bliss.

I have in my life been reluctantly present on two occasions as a juvenile at adult rowing races, each occasion bringing with it its own little moment of personal disaster. The first one was indeed at Henley. We lived at the time in Berkshire and kind friends, inviting me to a summer picnic, failed to preface the word 'picnic' with the adjective 'boating'. Had they done so, instant refusal and for a reason that I will shortly supply, would have been the result. However, once I had accepted, there was no backing out. Cars deposited us at some Thames-side boathouse or other and we were rapidly settled in various craft and moored alongside some floating piece of wood (can it be called a 'boom'?) beyond which the merry rowers were to row. We had with us assorted liquids. We had one of those enormously heavy, wedding-present wicker picnic hampers stuffed with indispensable lunch items such as cold salmon. We had, too, Miss Gertrude Lawrence, if only in circular wax form and on a gramophone record and singing a Gershwin number called 'Do Do Do' which blared forth, unmindful of the musical tastes of our neighbours, from an HMV red leather portable requiring constant cranking. And in next to no time at all, I began to feel seasick. Craft of varying displacements surged to and fro upon the water and the odious boat in which I sat was never at rest.

This really outstanding talent to be sick in any circumstances, however unpromising, and on every occasion, however improbable, had been with me since quite a little tot and it continued well into youth and never let me down. It was a talent equal to any challenge. To be sick in omnibuses, motorcars, trains, taxis and the underground was, of course, mere child's play. I had been splendidly sick on the roundabout at a fair, and I had managed some spectacular heavings after bicycling rather too speedily over a humpback bridge. I had twice been sick during sermons, a great gain, and had been happily hurried out. I had been sick, for no known reason but excitement, over the front row of the dress circle of the dear old

King's Theatre, Hammersmith, during the matinee of a panto-mime ('What's that on your hat, Sylvia?'). So to be sick at Henley presented no sort of problem to a gift such as mine and the oars of the winning crew of the next race received, as they flashed by, an unexpected and colourful pink tribute. In closing I will just say that to be sick at Henley does not make for wide popularity.

My next presence at competitive rowing took place at Cambridge where, to aid me in my mastery of the German language, I had an admirable supervisor called Miss Wilkinson, a lady of, compared with mine, fairly mature years and whose entire emotional life seemed to be centred on a small female dog. The dog's breed was far from clearly defined but it looked as though it came from some remote section of the mysterious East and it bore, in its whiskery and watery-eyed way, quite a resemblance to the wife of Dr Fu Manchu. Its name was Kurt, which your knowledge of English, if not of German, will tell you means 'short'. Kurt is, in fact, a male German Christian name, as we know from its connection with Weill, but it suffered here a sex-change, or possibly its canine owner was modishly bisexual. Short indeed she was, if not positively stunted, and looked not unlike a ball of brown wool that had started to unravel. Kurt went everywhere with Miss Wilkinson and I was not surprised to find her present in the car when dear Miss W arranged for us a picnic à deux during May. Here again, the fact that it was to be a river picnic was concealed from me, though fortunately we remained in this case on dry land. Miss Wilkinson, conscientiously larding her conversation with German phrases to help me in my oral work, had wrongly assumed that I would wish to watch the college rowing races, a feature of May Week, and so we sat at some central point of the river bank where the boats were assembling and, while dispensing delicious food and drink (chilled Hock, naturally), she asked me to point out my college boat. Alas, I couldn't. I had not the very faintest idea which it was and Miss Wilkinson was giving me rather a reproachful look when there was, fortunately, a diversion.

We had both of us underestimated the power of nature and of Mrs Fu Manchu. Tiring of our company, Kurt had wandered off and had found new friends and was now the centre of a laughing four-legged group. She obviously had an allure which, though not immediately apparent to the human eye,

*We're too late (Wir sind zu spät)*

rendered her in the canine world the Jean Harlow of the river bank. *Troublante* she was. There used to be in those days, and perhaps there still is, a dog repellent called Keep Away, or some such name – an ointment which you applied to doggie where it would do most good. Miss Wilkinson, the picture of innocence, had plainly never heard of Keep Away. Neither Goethe nor Schiller made the slightest mention of Keep Away. Nobody in Lessing's immensely boring plays ever went out to buy a jumbo tin of Keep Away. None of those tuneful *lieder* touched on the stuff.

It was clear that to keep anybody, let alone an exciting new friend, away from her was Kurt's last intention. Her behaviour can only be described as obliging. What are friends for, she seemed to be thinking, but to be obliged? By the time we realised what was happening, had risen from the grass and had hastened to her side, Kurt was obliging a third friend, a vast bulldog which, though ill suited to her, was managing splendidly. Miss Wilkinson bravely disentangled Kurt from her current paramour and let out a wild cry of 'We're too late'. But even then, at this crisis moment, she remembered (*'Wir sind zu spät'*) to translate it, bless her, into German.

# Christmas crackers

Opposed as I am to almost all forms of change and sadly noting in the modern world this or that alteration or withdrawal of an amenity (drinking-troughs for horses, for example, always such a pleasing and watery attraction in a town's main street), I much regret the total disappearance in large shops of floor-walkers. These tall and black-jacketed gentlemen, who all looked like reputable Victorian cabinet ministers, were especially numerous in Selfridges and, sighting a customer, would come gliding smoothly forward, anxious to help. You stated your requirement ('Winter vests, please, chest 42'), upon which, and to a cry of 'Forward please, Miss Babbacombe', you were wafted to the right counter and offered a chair to sit on (chairs have also disappeared, and even counters seem to be on the way out and those square loose-boxes curtly labelled PAY HERE are not the same thing at all). And I find deeply depressing the notice saying THIEVES WILL BE PROSECUTED, which I always misread as PERSECUTED – much the same thing. There are certainly in Fortnum's, shop of shops, some men who *look* like floor-walkers but I have never liked, on my way to Preserves, to ask them if they are.

Quite a jolly game for the snug winter fireside, curtains drawn and nothing on the telly, is to suggest occupations that famous people might, judging solely by their exteriors, have been busy with if they hadn't been what they were, if you follow me, lucidity itself as usual. Thus, the enchanting little songbird, Edith Piaf, might have been taken for a pre-war boy or girl *ramasseuse* or picker-up of tennis balls at the equivalent of a bob an hour on the courts at Cannes. Goethe could, from the likenesses available and having the necessary gloomy face for it, easily have been an undertaker ('I've come to measure Herr Baumgarten up') and cheating a bit on the side too, with coloured and stained beech masquerading as oak. I see Mussolini as a rather shifty travel-agent, all toothy smiles over the bogus holiday brochures ('Benidorm it shall be then') and leaning over the counter the better to appreciate a neatly turned female ankle. Lloyd George was obviously a highly successful open-air auctioneer and Stanley Baldwin a genial bank manager, puffing that pipe and all confident smiles prior to refusing an overdraft at some such place as Staines. Mrs Baldwin, on the other hand, must surely have been a medium, professionally called 'Zara', hung with endless necklaces and chains for her trances and producing ectoplasm galore in a rather dingy bed-sit somewhere in the Earls Court area. And Arnold Bennett, with that splendid coif of hair and gold-chained waistcoat, can have been nothing else but a floor-walker, not one of your tall and smart and lissom Selfridges brand but a portly, friendly, supervising presence among the soft furnishings in a leading store at, say, Blackburn.

I cheerfully make you a present of the game (somebody names the character to be transmogrified and allots marks for the results) and, anxious as I am for all readers to shine this Christmas, I am also providing some back-up comedic material for you in case the humorous cracker riddles that come your way are not fully up to scratch. I see you being the life and soul, I really do, and you just can't miss with these. Practise them over a time or two in private and then away you go. I give them in a roughly descending order of merit though to some these conundra may seem to be of a uniform level of excellence. Question: 'If a farmer sold 70 per cent of his sheep for £8,000, what would the remaining 30 per cent realise?' Answer: 'They would realise that a lot of their friends had gone.' Q: 'What did the Spanish farmer say to his hens? A: 'Olé.' Q: 'What has four legs and a trunk?' A: 'A married couple going on holiday.' And just one more for luck, and one of those that may need explanation. Q: 'When is a bus like water?' A: 'When it is due (dew).' There!

To return for a space to the Blackburn floor-walker, had you ever realised that his first name was, like the Mr Powell of whom we now seem to hear so little, Enoch? This is the kind of fact that a mind as richly stocked as my own coughs up from time to time and at unexpected moments. Little nuggets of information that have been lurking there for ages suddenly come popping out. A number of mine tend to be theatrical tit-bits and only the other day and while reassuring Mrs

Mountjoy (Berenice in unbuttoned mood) about the improbability of Devon, let alone Appleton, ever suffering an earthquake ('If only we all lived in bungalows . . . !'), the figure of 2238 appeared as if by magic before my eyes. This, as many of you won't need reminding, is the number of performances achieved by *Chu-Chin-Chow* on its first production in 1916. Now what on earth can have jerked that out? The connection between underground rumblings and tuneful numbers such as 'Any Time's Kissing Time' is by no means immediately clear. And then only last Tuesday and while inspecting the ON OFFER section on proud display in our village shop (4p off tinned meat balls, a nutriment that never finds its way into the 'Myrtlebank' *cuisine* but which doubtless has its place in the Great Architect's scheme of things), I suddenly recalled and for no sensible reason a line from a production long ago of *Floradora* by the admirable Oundle Amateur Operatic Society in our spacious Victoria Hall. One of the minor characters uttered some thoughtful line or other about Life, to which her friend rather testily replied 'Don't be philosophical, Lottie.' Did you ever!

But however well stocked the mind, and mine is, as you see, exceptionally chock-a-block with intellectual treasures and the envy of many, one can always find a nook in it in which to harbour for future use this or that astonishing conversation-stopper, and a real stunner has recently come into my life concerning Elgar, and I do not need to add 'the composer' for all other Elgars seem to have been hiding their lights under bushels and only the one has, as far as I know, struggled gloriously to fame (said by some to have been at times *un peu difficile* but let that pass). I have garnered the fascinating Elgar fact from a far too long delayed reading of Osbert Sitwell's excellent *Noble Essences*, a series of personal recollections of such interesting and gifted people as Gosse, Firbank, Sickert, Rex Whistler and others. In his charming and adulatory piece on the noted, in two senses, harpsichordist, Violet Gordon Woodhouse, Sir Osbert relates that at a wartime gathering in the Woodhouses' flat in Mount Street, Mayfair, the eighty-seven-year-old Bernard Shaw, having walked all the way from Whitehall Court, announced, after a characteristic utterance of 'at my age you are either well or dead', that Elgar had liked to play, and over and over again, the gramophone records made by Cicely Courtneidge and Jack Hulbert, stating that in them he found the secret of the perfect use of rhythm. Did you, once again, ever! And just to think that if only I had moved in the right social circles, I could have been relishing this item for the best part of forty years.

Detective work is necessary here, for all must want to know which particular records so especially tickled Sir Edward's ear. The choice is not, as it happens, as wide as all that, for Elgar died in 1934 and the Hulberts, though in their different spheres already well enough known since about 1910, especially Miss Courtneidge (daughter of Robert Courtneidge, a sort of earlier C. B. Cochran), did not come into real prominence until, in 1923, the *Little Revue* at, where else, the Little Theatre, long since gone. By 1924 and another revue, the matchless *By The Way*, they were real stars, and so we have actually only ten years to cover. When did these dazzling talents first venture onto wax? Only the BBC record library could tell us, and I hardly like to thrust myself forward and make what might seem to them, with the strain of keeping Radio 3 so constantly provided with material, a trifling enquiry. So I must fall back on my own memory and resources and here I can be not unhelpful for in December 1926, the Hulberts appeared together at the Gaiety in a merry musical called *Lido Lady*.

Invited by my kind parents to name a theatrical treat for the Christmas hols, I looked no further than *Lido Lady*, where we found the Hulberts playing a brother and sister, Harry and Peggy Bassett, the former in love with Phyllis Dare, as was half the audience, and the latter happily affianced to Harold French, a delightful *jeune premier* soon to partner Gertrude Lawrence in *Oh, Kay!* and later to become (*French Without Tears*) a distinguished director. The piece was one of the earliest Rodgers and Hart hits and I still possess a recording, pressed, as we used then to say, in 1927 but as good as ever, give or take a few scratches, of a number rendered *con brio* by the Hulberts. It was called 'Try Again Tomorrow' and its lively lyric told the story of a rascally dance instructor who saw to it that his fee-paying pupils made little or no progress and remained, therefore, fee-paying. The number has a very rhythmic and pleasingly jiggy tune and the Hulberts, effortlessly enunciating and banging it out, gave it all they had, which was plenty. How astonished I would have been as I ceaselessly played this joyous record on my portable and jigged a little bit myself, to know that Sir Edward's, I suspect, stately mahogany 'Console' model was churning out the very same sounds, for who can doubt that this was one of the Hulbert records that he found so irresistible. Did he, when nobody was looking, jig a bit too? I do hope so.

# Chinese take-away

I have mentioned before in these pages, and with a deep gratitude that increases down the years, a married couple called Edwards who became an adopted aunt and uncle and who lavished kindnesses and love on me from 1922, when our paths first crossed, on. I had at that time, and aged twelve, as little to recommend me as I have now, when people, though too polite to shudder away, do tend suddenly to remember appointments elsewhere ('Is that the time? Heavens, I must fly!'). I suppose that I smiled quite a lot, which is socially more acceptable than frowning, but as a pleasing accomplishment it was a poor thing to compensate for selfishness, clumsiness, gluttony, lack of tact, boorishness and the many other unattractive disadvantages not always absent in young people growing up. I have sometimes wondered why on earth they bothered with me and I think it was perhaps because of a sad gap in their lives for their only child, a girl called May, had died young and of TB, and those who ceaselessly fret and fuss and complain about the undoubted horrors of modern life can cheer themselves up by running over in their minds the names of the numerous and appalling illnesses that exist no more or, existing, can be speedily cured. And when they've done that, they can become even sunnier by reflecting on the fact that, a mere forty-five years ago, many people in the country were, literally, starving and that now starvation is, for us at least, virtually a thing of the past. I have other comforting thoughts which I shall supply from time to time.

The Edwards, who lived in London (just off Kensington High Street and finely placed for Mudie's Library, Barkers, the Circle Line and that delightful No 9 bus), were tremendous theatre-goers who could be counted on to have seen 'everything', and often twice, and as, from the age of four, most of my waking moments and thoughts were concerned with this or that star performer, this formed an additional bond. Every school holidays I spent three or four days with them (comfy, roomy flat and with two servants, then nothing of a novelty, living in, and a married chauffeur living out) and it is to their kindness that I owe many prime theatrical treats, among them *No No Nanette*, Cochran revues, Marie Tempest and endless afternoons at the Coliseum where all the best music hall acts turned up.

The Edwards did not confine themselves on their theatre-going activities to London and often took themselves off for a few days to the South Coast where almost every town of any size had its theatre (many had two or more), complete either with a repertory company or a tour of some successful London production (*The Scarlet Pimpernel* and *The Only Way* made fortunes on the road, as we buskers have it). And one Sunday evening in the late 1920s and at, I think, Brighton, my friends spotted that a Special Concert was to be given, 'with a host of famous names', the names prudently not being announced until the audience had paid for their tickets and were actually in the hall, and seated. The Edwards hastened, naturally, to this promising-sounding feast and there a sadness awaited them, for one of the famous names was famous indeed. It is very distressing when a once great star is a star no more and plainly on the skids (wasn't it Mae Murray who was found, destitute and penniless and starving in a back street of Los Angeles?) and among the items in this Sunday concert there was 'songs by Hayden Coffin', a name which once shone out in what were then known as bulbs. For many years he had been an immensely popular leading singer and a handsome star of stars in such musicals as *Dorothy, A Gaiety Girl* (at, surprisingly, the Prince of Wales's), *The Geisha, The Quaker Girl, Véronique* and *A Country Girl*. His voice had, more or less, gone (he was by then in his 60s) but he did what he could with it and, when all was over, the Edwards hurried round to see and congratulate and, if it doesn't sound too patronising, comfort him. He was, they said, charm itself, accepted his vanished success with dignity and announced that the sum to be paid him for his evening's efforts had been agreed at two guineas.

He died a few years later, in 1935, and I shall always be grateful to him for having, in his 1930 autobiography, passed on to us details of a remarkable contraption, the very name of which sets one wildly surmising as to its purpose. I am referring, of course, to the Ammoniaphone, a boon that was introduced to a fascinated public at an Ammoniaphone Concert at the St James's Hall in 1884. It seems that the Ammoniaphone looked vaguely like a white metal flute and could apparently either be blown into head on, so to speak, or, like a flute, sideways. What dulcet sounds it produced we are not told but the inventor of the Ammoniaphone claimed that by dint of inhaling into the lungs various gases, and presumably ammoniacal ones, contained in the tube and which were identical, though how I cannot follow, with the pure air only obtainable in Italy, the home of beautiful voices, a greater richness and depth would be added to the vocal tones. At the Ammoniaphone Concert, the Ammoniaphone inventor blew a series of arpeggios and grace notes and trills vigorously into his instrument, though whether he then sang in order to demonstrate his improved cords is not revealed. It was well known to the Victorians, never very quick to spot an obvious and complete charlatan, that ammonia, the pungent compound of nitrogen and hydrogen, was invaluable for washing your navy blue linens or freshening your velvets, but here was a brand new use for it and, apparently, eager buyers flocked to the Ammoniaphone shop in Oxford Street to purchase their very own Ammoniaphone. Although I have searched the Army and Navy Catalogue without success, something tells me that somewhere in Harrods there is an Ammoniaphone counter and I intend to stock up with Ammoniaphones (the ideal answer to the Christmas present problem) at once.

It is not forgotten by some of us that Hayden Coffin also appeared in a musical called *San Toy* (Chinesey, and with Marie Tempest as leading lady) at Daly's, a musical for which, though before my time, I have, for a peculiar reason, a warm feeling. Early in my teaching career, I was appointed a House Tutor, or under-Housemaster, at an Oundle School boarding house. There were, it being the 30s, a large assembly of housemaids to look after us and, passing through the boys' quarters one evening, I heard a strange sighing sound and a clatter of limbs and I found to my dismay that one of the maids, Rhoda by name, had, returning from her evening out, decided to faint rather elaborately and now lay, a sad and forlorn human mound, upon the floor and in full public view. I hastened, in my gentlemanly way, forward, heaved Rhoda up as best I could and, clutching her firmly, was just wondering what best to do with her inert form when the whole of the junior half of the house passed by on their way up to bed. When this kind of thing used to occur in plays and, particularly, farces, the stage direction that followed this kind of happening just said TABLEAU. The little affair made quite a talking point for a number of weeks.

There was, in *San Toy*, a narrative song – one of those that tells a story, such as Cole Porter's 'Miss Otis Regrets' and Mr Coward's 'Nina' – concerning Rhoda Rye, described as a London lass, 'taking and trim and tiny, who wished to gather the upper class to a tea-shop charming and Chinee'. Rhoda, the lyric tells us, then erected a pagoda in the Strand and dressed up in Chinese costume, complete with comb. After this preamble, there came the chorus.

> Rhoda, Rhoda ran a Pagoda
> Selling tea and syrup and soda,
> Many a maiden met a man
> At the pretty Pagoda Rhoda ran.

*when the whole of the junior half of the house passed by on their way up to bed. . . .*

It was, clearly, the first instance of a Chinese take-away, except that what male customers took away was on two legs, and alive.

You'll want to know what happened to Rhoda Rye herself. Well, she got snapped up by none other than the Duke of Kensington Gardens, a constant visitor to her Pagoda, became his Duchess and pretended that she had never in her life even *heard* of a Pagoda. But what eventually happened to my Rhoda, I cannot, alas, say.

# Foolish things

I have made so bold in the past as to share with you, and at least twice before, my experiences while trying to find a mate, that elusive Miss Right who side-steps and dodges me for all the world as though she played rugger for England and who, in my fevered imagination, is a sort of joyous amalgam of Garbo (extreme beauty allied to not too much in the way of chat), Mrs Beeton (tasty tuck), F. Nightingale (succour in illness) and Dorothy Parker (quips galore and a breezy approach to life). But what, staunch feminists not a million miles from here will be demanding, have I to offer in return, particularly after setting my sights (Garbo, indeed!) so unjustifiably high? Precious little, must be my answer. Few teeth, though all my own. A dislike of parsnips in any form. No trust at all in God or in prayer (I sometimes think that the batteries in His hearing-aid have long since conked out). A tendency to read little that is new but to re-read for the umpteenth time imperishable treats such as *Decline and Fall*, *The Enchanted April*, *David Copperfield* and every novel by Stella Gibbons. Not very much to put in the shop window, I do admit.

I do not mention the name of Garbo without careful thought for Fate's Whirligig, obviously in madcap mood, once accorded me a meeting, though a brief one, with this goddess. It was in 1956 and she was for a short while in London masquerading as 'Miss Brown' and deceiving almost nobody. I was working at the time in Cambridge and as secretary, eye-shade and both my typing fingers at the ready, to Lord Rothschild. The latter was a friend of Miss G and a car was to be sent to London to collect her from the Savoy Hotel and bring her back to Cambridge for lunch. The house's drive was fairly narrow and to get her to the front door the car would have to pass the window of the room where I worked. I had a word with the ever obliging chauffeur and begged him to drive by as slowly as possible so that I could have a proper look at this unique performer.

He did even better than that. He stopped altogether and Miss G, evidently thinking that she had arrived, peered through the car window to see where she was. A light rain had been falling, that superb face was untouched by time and at once we were back again in those marvellous scenes in the early talkie of *Anna Christie* where, a bemacintoshed figure in a drab felt hat, she haunted the damp dockside and looked about, I am very sorry to have to remind you but facts are facts and must be faced, for men. Hollywood's puritanism being what it was in the early 30s, it wasn't made all that clear what she was up to but the more nimble-minded could at once spot her profession although she was of course, underneath it all and in the very best traditions of fictional prostitutes, as pure as the driven snow and with a heart of gold. And there, after all these years, she was once more, raindrops, wistful look and all, and not four feet away from me. Later in the day, my kind employer made an excuse to send for me and I positively met her. Firm hand-shake. Huge feet. Slight smile. Silence. Anxious to get, so to speak, a close-up, I advanced my face perilously near to hers and she, interested I suppose to see what strange English fish stood before her, did the same thing. Our noses didn't actually touch but it was a very close thing. Please to forgive this boastful snippet and take comfort from the fact that ever since that peak moment my life has been just one long *dégringolade*.

But back to a possible Miss Right. Although I am obviously no great cop either physically or mentally, it is true that I have commodious 'Myrtlebank' to lay, as it were, at her feet and those who say that it would not be ethical to dazzle her with such an outstanding architectural attraction are tàlking through their hats. She'll want to know where she's going to live, won't she? Well then. February does not find us, I fear, at our tippy-topmost best horticulturally but I shall be able to show her where the arum lilies will be when they decide to pop up, and explain to her that the large supply of dead brown stalks in the ground will one glorious day be fuchsias again.

I have been trying to relate Miss Right to some of the lyrics in that well-known song 'These Foolish Things', now made available to us in John Hadfield's splendidly catholic *Everyman's Book of English Love Poems* and bless me if Garbo doesn't, like my arums, come popping up again: 'The smile of Garbo and the scent of roses,/The waiters whistling as the last bar closes'. I don't exactly envisage my Miss Right with mock Mona Lisa leer reeling tipsily out of the Appleton pub long after 'Time' has been called and smelling strongly of stout, but I can perhaps throw a little light on the line that goes 'The sigh of midnight trains in empty stations'. The lyricist is here plainly referring to the 10.15 p.m. from Paignton which reaches and passes through Torquay at about 10.55 p.m., not midnight precisely but poetic licence and all that (no buffet car facilities, and change at Newton Abbot). The line that rhymes with this timely praise of the varied charms of British rail is 'Silk stockings thrown aside, dance invitations'. Nothing is less inviting than untidiness in bedrooms and the place for silk stockings, though I tend to see Miss Right in nylon or, even, tights, is a drawer. As to the dance invitations, here we must wait for the Bultitudes and what they call their yearly 'hop' and which is sometimes a fancy dress one, with Giles as a pirate waving a Jolly Roger (shrieks of 'Where's the rum, me hear-ties?' and a chance to pinch a bottom or two) and Bunty as a wildly animated Dresden shepherdess.

The song contains other and more worrying lines. 'A cigarette that bears a lip-stick's traces' implies a regular resort to gaspers (younger readers may care to learn that that is the word that some of us golden oldies used to use for our fags). 'Gardenia perfume' and 'long excited cables' hint at an ex-travagance well beyond my pocket, and as for 'wild strawber-ries', these are mentioned as being 'only seven francs a kilo'. 'Only' indeed! This works out at about eleven shillings and eightpence the punnet. The engagement is off.

# Serpent's teeth

My father had a theory, not solidly based on any actual motoring experience on the road, that cars ran much better at night-time than by day. Returning from some outing and nearing home just as dusk was falling, he would listen appreciatively to the unchanging hum of the engine and say 'ah, it scents the evening air.' Whether this was a conscious but altered quotation from that sad spectre, the ghost of Hamlet's father and his 'But, soft! methinks I scent the morning air; Brief let me be', I do not know and it was certainly not the kind of question that one would have put to him. A counter-question would have resulted ('Why do you ask?'). I merely used to wonder if, in the unlikely and unwelcome event of a drive with my father right through the night, he would, when dawn came up, notice a sudden roughness in the engine's running.

From the 1920s on, the car we had was invariably a Morris (and during affluent years there were two), beginning with a bull-nosed Morris Cowley complete with hideously exposed and uncomfortable dickey seat, and progressing (wasn't there once a brand with a chassis rather daringly called a 'chummy body'?) through various models to a sedate Morris Oxford which had beige curtains to the windows, was painted a depressing dark brown and always seemed to me to bè indistinguishable from a hearse. One felt one should be lying flat, embowered in blooms and deafened by sobs. But whatever sort we currently had, they were all alleged keenly to enjoy travel by night. As to the 'Brief let me be', this was never part of my father's creed. If a thing was worth saying, it was therefore worth saying at considerable length. Fortunately for him, he was quite unaware of both boredom and ruffled feathers in others ('Why did Miss Manning leave so early?').

For all trips by car we departed a full hour before we need, in case of accidents and unforeseen delays. There might, one never knew, be a puncture. There might be a nose-bleed requiring prostration and a cold key down the back. We might be witnesses of some exciting happening (murder, rape, robbery, regicide) and the police would need our names and lively recollections. Somebody might faint, and there was always a flask of brandy and some smelling-salts on board. Both of these emergency kit items led in their day, as did so many of the would-be kindly acts performed by my father, to misunderstandings and angry red faces and umbrage. We were once passing a pub and, seeing a man propped up, seated, against a wall with his eyes shut, my father instantly assumed that he had fainted. He leapt from the car, rushed forward with the smelling-salts and thrust them up the man's nose. But it was only a tipsy local who had been enjoying a quiet nap and who was understandably furious at being thus interfered with and so sharply recalled from the Land of Nod. My father had to make a somewhat hasty return to the car, pursued by a volley of exciting oaths which I did not at the time understand, and questions only produced 'Hush, dear'.

And another time, near Aldershot, we saw a trooper being unseated from his prancing horse, and, falling to the ground, lying motionless and as though dead. My father darted out with the flask and poured brandy down the man's throat (loud splutterings), only to be turned on by a wrathful officer who came galloping up. The trooper, he shouted, might have choked: he might have severe internal injuries for which brandy could be lethal, etc etc. It took quite a lot to abash my father but the officer, accustomed by his profession to dispense abuse where needed, succeeded splendidly and my father, in a cricketing term, retired hurt ('I only wanted to help'). To lighten the occasion, my mother, a great soother and a calm presence during many of Life's turbulences, produced some patum pepperium sandwiches, that delicious salty and fishy substance that is also known as Gentleman's Relish (can the trade name now have been changed to Gentleperson's Relish?) and quite soon we all cheered up. Tomato soup and halibut (taken separately, I hasten to say) had also been known in their time to soothe my father when soothing was required at home, though at home it tended to be our visitors who needed the soothing.

There are, sadly, two things in life that can never be taught. One is 'timing' in acting, especially comedy. The other is tact.

They are instinctive matters and are either present or not. The absence of tact in one or both parents was a subject that I frequently discussed in youth with my friend, Williamson, at our prep school on the Hampshire coast. Williamson was, if I may just remind you, the boy with whom I discovered the facts of life, more or less, with the aid of some striking wall drawings in the gentlemen's retiring-room of a rather scruffy and open air service rifle-range (much used in the first world war) and which lay within Sunday walking distance of our school. A few minor details were, I see now, missing but the drawings gave us the general spirit of the thing and indicated what to aim at in due course. The need constantly to refresh our memories and examine any fresh pictures made Sunday afternoons busier than ever. There was much to be done. Sunday letters home to dash off and cheer our loved ones ('Willoughby was sick in

*a charming but over-emotional mother*

church'). Potatoes to be collected, sometimes with the cook's permission, from the kitchen (we used, permanently hungry, to make wood fires and bake them in the ashes). Then a quick look at Williamson's signed photograph of Dorothy Dickson and a discussion, fed on gossipy sections of the weekly *Sketch* and *Bystander*, as to how she might be spending her Sunday (brunch at Bray with Gerald du Maurier, we often assumed). Then a peppermint-cream or perhaps a pear-drop, after which it was heigh-ho for the range, two miles away but, like so many items in Baedeker, worth *le détour*.

Boys in the two top forms were allowed on Sundays to wander abroad at will, provided that they went in twos, and at the range we lit, after a peep or two at the sensational graffiti, our twig fire and baked the potatoes. On the way back we used to call at a small shop, obligingly open on Sundays, which sold cigarettes and were usually able to persuade the proprietor to ferret about in the unsold packets in search of cigarette cards (Wildflowers of Britain. Characters of Dickens) that we needed for our sets. And so, exhausted, to tea (bread, margarine, jam and a bubbling urn, the ensemble presided over by Matron), followed by another peppermint-cream and a further glance at Dorothy Dickson (by now, we supposed, sipping champagne and having supper with Jack Buchanan).

We always referred, for some reason, to our parents as 'people'. 'My people are coming down on Saturday' one would say in an elaborately offhand manner, praying that one's mother's hat would not cause comment or that one's father would not be too ebullient with the headmaster ('How's the young man coming along?'). Williamson too had his worries – a charming but over-emotional mother who was given to embracing him publicly rather more often than we considered needful, and a delightfully round and bouncey dad permanently a-chuckle whom Williamson found bothersome but whom I thought, disloyally, to be the nicest kind of father. Did either Williamson or myself ever feel a spark of gratitude for the fact that we were being relatively expensively educated and, provided we worked reasonably hard, led a completely trouble-free life? No we did not. Did we ever pause to consider, as one passed slum dwellings in London and other towns, what our unhappy lot as children might have been? No we did not. Williamson, having an altogether nicer character than I, never actually criticised his parents but I, odious and fault-finding and whining, droned ceaselessly on about my father's border-line imperfections and the agitating nature of some features of my home life. One took food, houses, pleasures, clothes, warmth, holidays, cars, books, toys and even, I am very sorry to say, love as being merely one's right. I cannot imagine why my parents didn't, at least twice a day, take my horrid little head and bang it violently against the nearest wall.

# Sister sleuths

The older I become, and as joyous year succeeds, with ever increasing rapidity, to joyous year, the less I approve of those who, with either the written or the spoken word, go in for really wholesale denigration of everybody and everything. This is hardly the place, and my goodness me it isn't, to name various individuals who seem to prefer to strike a sour note, but for me the journalistic scene has never been the same since the demise, and I think it must have been a pre-war death, of the dear old *Happy Magazine*, jammed with fun and pun and japes and general jollity, with an especially merry line in jokes and illustrations of honeymoon couples setting off for Brighton in a car whose numberplate read OU2. Reluctant as I am ever to criticise in the smallest degree either Americans or the land in which they live (I have asked you before now to picture a world without America. Very well then, kindly go right ahead and picture it all over again), the USA did produce a literary gentleman who went in quite a bit for denigration and who chose to disparage two of my favourite manufacturers of highly saleable and readable prose.

The gentleman concerned was Edmund Wilson. Snaps of him reveal no fun figure. The face is gloomy. Secret sorrows seem to lurk. He may well have smiled, say, every other year but I have seen no visual evidence of it. Anyhow, this Mr Wilson decided to speak patronisingly, at best, of Somerset Maugham's abilities as a writer of short stories (I would have thought it clear to all that, in addition to *Rain*, there are at least half a dozen of the longer stories which are masterpieces of their kind), before moving on, horrid old toad, to attempt to demolish Agatha Christie and the detective story in general in an article called, if I've remembered it correctly, 'Who cares who killed Roger Ackroyd?'

Well, I do for one, and with me her vast and worldwide

readership, from South Sea Islanders goggling away in, naturally, the south, to Eskimos way beyond the timber line and in the frozen arctic, for who can doubt that after a nourishing supper of *surprise de reindeer* and before lights out in the igloo, Mrs Christie is excitedly passed, in translation, from hand to hand and devoured in the feeble glow from the whale-blubber lamp, though one does rather wonder what Miss Marple's muffins and seedcake and uncle (Canon of Ely) come out as in Eskimo. Devoted Christie readers will recall demure Jane Marple as being a charmingly fluttery, dithery, feathery spinster and cottage-resident in the village of St Mary Mead (the very name breathes gentility), a fitting background for a character whose apparent innocuousness and lack of grasp lulls murderers galore into the fatal mistake of underrating her and her remarkable powers of detection and deduction. But I doubt whether either Mrs Christie or the dear little creature herself ever realised what a problem they pose for imaginative readers who also dwell in reputable villages.

Let us, for example, suppose that I have just re-read one of the many marvellous Miss Marple crime stories. Emerging from 'Myrtlebank' and into the peaceful roads of Appleton, I make for one of the village shops and encounter, en route, Mrs Mountjoy (Berenice at moments of conviviality). She is alone. Odd! No sign of the Canon. 'Where's Roland?' I say in my cheery way, adding merrily 'Done him in at last?' Berenice, obviously flustered, looks guilty and blushes (not much sense of humour there, I fear) and little more is needed to convince me that at that moment the Canon is lying dead on his library floor with an eastern dagger of curious design buried up to the hilt between his shoulder blades. In his left hand are the galoshes which he was prudently about to slip on, for the day is inclement, and his right hand clutches a torn piece of paper on which is written 'Vim, Harpic, Daz, toilet rolls, Airwick freshener, post *Church Times* and collect pension', words which the naive and uninitiated will immediately take to be a shopping-list but which, to a Marple mind, are important and full of hidden significance.

Then I meet, to cries of 'What ho, chaps!', Giles Bultitude just climbing into the Merc and heavy with expensive purchases (we now boast a delicatessen counter). No sign of Bunty. Strange! Dead as a doornail, I can only suppose, spreadeagled on the luxi-duvet in the master suite and suffocated by one of those voluminously-crinolined ladies who, in some bedrooms, conceal the upstairs telephone. In her death struggles, she has pluckily managed to seize a biro and scratch on the telephone pad just three letters of an uncompleted word – CRI. Was it the name of her murderer, 'Crittenden' or 'Critchley'? Was she, possibly, trying to express surprise and dismay at her demise with the mild oath of 'Crikey!'? Was it perhaps a thoughtful reminder, a devoted wife to the last, to Giles that they are fresh out of crinkle cut potatoes, a 'Spar' speciality? Having no local Miss Marple, we shall never know.

Those devoted literary researchers down the less well-trodden paths, Patricia Craig and Mary Cadogan (remember their *You're a Brick, Angela!*, a splendid review of girls school stories?) have been at it again and to our great profit. *The Lady Investigates* (Gollancz, £9.95) features fictional women detectives and spies in rich profusion and from both sides of the Atlantic. The names alone are fascinating – Nora Van Snoop (terribly unconventional and dined at the Café Royal alone, if you please), the old maidish Amelia Butterworth (her murderers included one who used a hat-pin and pushed his victims down wells, just like Lady Audley) and a lady unfortunately called Clarice Dyke, happily married, however, and to a male detective, so that's all right. There was also the intrepid Eileen Dare who jumped off the top of blazing buildings rather more successfully than they did in *The Towering Inferno* and who was sometimes trapped in London cellars with the Thames flood water rising about her ('Oh, what a state my costume will be in!'). And on to the wonderfully hearty Mrs Pym who discovers a woman stabbed to death in a boat and just says 'Lug her to the bank and we'll have a look-see.'

As to spies, there is even a French one in a Biggles story (wildly inefficient, she allows her carrier pigeon to get eaten by a cat), while that great authority, Bernard Newman, speaks admiringly of a real life lady of easy virtue called Regina who was able to blink messages accurately in Morse code. Ideal for husbands and wives at dull dinner parties ('How soon can we leave?').

# Day by day

It is only very rarely that I am able, tucked away as I am in my cosy Devonian backwater, to bring readers a stimulating titbit of news, but every so often I chance, in my wide reading, to come upon something worth passing on, although the titbit that I am about to stagger you with dates back, I am afraid, to the year 1932, a year already made memorable for us by the consecration of Buckfast Abbey by Cardinal Bourne and by the opening of the Sydney Harbour Bridge, such a well loved tribute to engineering skills down under. But for all that it is forty-seven years old, my titbit is none the less surprising for that. Indeed, the word 'titbit' is quite inadequate for this sensational item and I have no hesitation in changing the description (and please do so too in your minds) to that of either 'bombshell' or 'grenade', so explosively exciting is it.

Ready? In April, 1932, there was produced at the New Theatre in London (a handsome theatre now known, by way of a compliment to a splendid theatrical entrepreneur family, as The Albery) a play called *Napoleon: The Hundred Days*. It was translated from a foreign lingo and adapted for the English stage by none other than John Drinkwater, who would have been happy indeed if the play had remained at the New and earned royalties for even fifty days, let alone a hundred, but the public unfortunately decided that a fortnight of this dramatic treat was quite sufficient. 'Translated', you note, but even if I tell you that the original language of the play was Italian, would you be any nearer to guessing the author? Stand well back while I pull out the pin, for the author was Mussolini. There now! By 1932 he had evidently got the Italian railways running to time and was therefore free to devote himself to literary work.

Did he, one so wonders, attend rehearsals? Was he to be seen at lunchtime wolfing ravioli among the theatrical world at the

Ivy Restaurant ('Why, hullo there, Noël!')? Did he, at the première, lurk at the back of the stalls, as playwrights are apt to do, and start the applause? Did he shower any actresses in the cast with costly blooms ('Oh but Benny, you shouldn't have!')? The mists have closed. All, alas, that we know is that he decorated the presenter of the play, Sydney Carroll, though here again we do not know with what he decorated him. Something metallic, probably which doubtless patriotic Mr Carroll caused to be melted down in 1940 and then subsequently dropped, in bomb form, on the donor.

It was not the first Napoleon to be seen, however briefly, at the New Theatre for in 1929 I well recall a merry piece there called *Madame Plays Nap* ('Nap' being, in this case, chummy for Napoleon) in which no less a person than Dame Sybil Thorndike herself, seizing a chance to show admirers of St Joan her more skittish side, played a merry piece indeed called Citizeness Pawnbroker who, though firmly married, flirted dottily with the Emperor in an unlikely series of wild and weird goings-on and in which Dame Sybil, not always the most restrained of players, overacted her generous heart out. Her husband, Lewis Casson, played Nap and was to be seen gazing quizzically at her throughout, as well he might. The billboards outside the theatre announced the play as being 'A continuous scream', the persons responsible for tempting the public with such an advertisement evidently having forgotten that, in addition to laughter, it is also possible to scream with horror.

Although in the field of tyrants and general wickedness, nothing and nobody could possibly be nastier than Hitler, Mussolini made a stab at excelling him and managed, in addition, to be both craven and utterly contemptible, in a way that Hitler never perhaps quite was. If my thoughts seem to be currently directed towards these two prominent noncharmers ('both of them are top of my shit list' Maurice Bowra used, and rather too robustly and outspokenly for some, to boom in public places), it is because there has recently come my way an absorbing wartime diary by a Mrs Milburn. Finding herself, a middle-class and happily married woman resident in the Midlands, at the beginning of hostilities bewailing the joining up of her only child, a much loved son who was, after Dunkirk, to become to prisoner of war for the duration, Mrs Milburn resolved to keep a day by day record of events in her life, both great and small, with walks for the dog, Twink, rightly getting as much space as some foreign events ('Molotov has lunched with Hitler!').

The moment when she finds that her son, reported missing, is, although wounded, all right, is very moving ('My darling dear, you are alive!') but not very often does she give way ('I brimmed over') to emotion for there is, goodness knows, so much to be done. The blackout to see to (material purchased in Leamington), Hitler to ponder on ('How he sleeps at night I can't think'), the world situation to be noted ('We are trying to soothe Japan'), telegrams to be sent to the Prime Minister ('Declare war on the treacherous Bordeaux Government' and signed 'Mrs Milburn'), going to the right sources for information ('Our position was lucidly and fully explained in *The Times* editorial'), and trying not to mistake the whining of greyhounds at a local kennel for the early notes of the air-raid siren. And every so often there was a daring and pleasurable trip to London ('Of course I left my gas mask in the taxi . . . and so to Harvey Nichols for lunch').

The view of life is, as you see, that taken by many good, solid, fearless Englishwomen of the period and of all classes. There is an occasional explosion of rage ('Pah!!!') but on the whole there is both a quiet acceptance of discomforts and a complete certainty of ultimate victory. Meanwhile there were her duties as school-manager, church services to be constantly attended, sometimes by torch light when the electricity was off, requests from Lord Woolton 'to go carefully with the tin opener', Women's Institute functions, lectures on gas warfare, references to the Italians as Wops, leeks at 4½d each and incomprehensible Irish plays on the wireless ('We shut it off and did the jig-saw awhile').

Foreigners mostly get very short shrift. Hess, parachuted into Scotland and slightly damaged, was said to be progressing well in hospital ('as if one cared'), and his whole trip by plane is summed up as 'gross impertinence'. Then there was Russia, of whom one didn't know just what to make ('her ways are not our ways'). The ex-Duce, reported to have vamoosed to Germany, is briskly dismissed as 'that bombastic idiot'. False German broadcasts about successes on the Russian front are greeted with 'M'yes!'. A particularly transparent lie by Hitler becomes 'a great big whopper', and the Germans fare invariably badly ('a nasty race indeed'). All Mrs Milburn's friends knew exactly what to do if invaders landed ('Mrs Whitaker is

*Mrs Whittaker is going to make them a cup of coffee and poison it if they ever call at the rectory*

going to make them a cup of coffee and poison it if they ever call at the Rectory'). So much for all that church-going! Love they neighbour doesn't seem to have caught on as a motto ('They talk of hanging all the Gestapo. Hurrah!'), and Mussolini has by now become 'that fat pomposity'.

Naturally there is throughout much preoccupation with food. The verger, doubtless weak from under-nourishment, faints at early service. The garden onions are found to have been attacked by the dreaded onion fly ('particularly vexing'). A chilly reception is given to eatables called Prem, Spam, Tang and Mor, and she allows herself an occasional outing (lunch at Coventry's Geisha Cafe and a matinee of *Gone With The Wind*). But in general food is no longer any sort of pleasure ('Toad-in-the-hole is *not* what it was').

*Mrs Milburn's Diaries* are admirably edited by Peter Donnelly and are published by Harrap at £6.95. They have a tragic ending. Her son duly returned to her from the prison camp, married happily and became the father of two children. And then, one morning in 1959 he was involved in a car accident on his way to work, an accident that was no fault of his, and died from his injuries. His mother, appalled at the waste of a life that had been preserved with some difficulty, did not long survive him, or would have wished to. I mention this just in case any reader decides, as a result, to drive a little more slowly and to take just that little bit more care.

# Man about town

As a really ardent film-goer with sixty-three years of devoted attendance and several million feet of celluloid behind me, I have never quite been able to decide which oft-repeated film cliché has been my very top favourite. I greatly enjoy the one in which a small mixed party of whiter than white British big game hunters is marooned somewhere among hostile natives and in dense jungle territory (in cheaper films the jungle was unmistakably Richmond Park, but never mind). War drums have been distantly thudding but these have now died away and the leader of the group, Colonel Merridew, narrows his eyes and says 'I don't like this silence'. Then, after a dusky head with what looks like an indelible pencil horizontally through its nose, has suddenly popped up from behind a bush, the fuzzy-wuzzies attack and the leading lady is swept up and carried off, still wearing her solar topee and waggling her legs up and down at high speed to register both anxiety and displeasure. She never, and how dramatically exciting it would have been, went into the cooking-pot to form the tasty main *plat* (*gigot de Mrs Merridew aux herbes*) for a black banquet, but there, you can't have everything.

Then there is the cliché when the hero, escaping from a rascally gang of international crooks (thin black moustaches and yellow faces much to the fore), goes flying down corridors and through windows and over roofs and eventually bursts through a door that leads to freedom, only to find that he has blundered by mistake into the central den itself of these arch-fiends, one of whom then steps forward (quite often it was Conrad Veidt) and says suavely 'Ah, come in, my dear Mr Henderson, ve haf been vaitink for you.' And then there are those innumerable poker games that end in, to put it mildly, displays of bad temper with the table overturned and guns blazing and everybody as cross as cross and a frightful old toothless pappy going 'Yippee' with excitement. For these disturbances we are usually in a remote saloon bar in some such outlandish spot as Broken Gibbet Gulch, a stone's throw from that, in films, constantly-named aquatic feature, the Sweet Water Canal (can there somewhere be, I ask myself, a Smelly Water Canal?).

Hitherto several things in life that were common knowledge to others, and poker games in particular, have been a complete mystery to me, never having known or bothered to find out whether two kings were better than an ace and three tens, or whatever. Not that such paltry hands ever appeared much in films. There, as far as one was allowed to see what they were holding, the better gamblers often seemed to have come by five aces, which surely can't be right.

Perceptive readers (and which NS subscriber is not?) will have pounced on that word I used, 'hitherto', and will perhaps have started to ask themselves whether I now know the rules of poker, whether I have actually started to play, and whence comes, so late in the day, this fresh blossoming, this new and sophisticated life-style. I shall, in due course and as is my way, explain all but let me first say that I have never been absolutely clear in my mind as to the actual meaning of 'sophisticated'. Perhaps you will help me to judge from the following incident. Many years ago, when staying in the South of France and at a time when that coastline was at the very height of its chic (more than I was), I was taken one day to a lunch party. I can never incidentally, get either my tongue or my pen happily round that word 'luncheon'. It makes me sound pretentious (do those who make use of the handy word 'brunch' ever, I wonder, think of it as being Bruncheon?). To name some of my fellow guests at this gathering would seem boastful and so I will suppress them. We were about thirty strong, and partly French.

Our hostess was a titled lady of considerable charm, distinction and wealth. It was high summer with the temperature in the eighties but her staff (the lady herself must have been consulted but can hardly have been very intimately concerned with such mundane matters) had arranged for us to sit at tables for four in bright sunlight on a shadeless terrace and there eat, unbelievable but true, piping hot veal rissoles nestling in a rich gravy and flanked by mashed potatoes, the dishes being handed to us by liveried footmen wearing white gloves. Struggling with the food, the rivers of sweat and the frog conversation ('*Aimez-vous Nice?*'), I looked about for our hostess, only to find that she was not among those present, having left fairly briskly, I was later told, for a different and obviously more agreeable lunch party further along the coast. This way of going on seemed very smart and dashing at the time, but was the lady's behaviour sophisticated or just plain bad manners? My dictionary says that 'sophisticated' includes 'qualities produced by special knowledge'. Well, she certainly had special and prior knowledge of those rissoles.

And it is special knowledge of a wide variety of subjects, poker included, that I am now pretty strong on. It comes from a book eagerly snapped up at, of all things, a Highgate jumble sale. Its owner can only have let it go in a blind moment of madness, or perhaps he had died, for it provides, for those males with ambitious but timorously shuffling social steps such as mine, a splendid passport to the *beau monde*. Here, surely, sits sophistication. Take, for instance, the book's first half, called, quite simply, 'Man About Town' and wafting us timewise straight back into a Wooster world. Riffling excitedly through the packed pages, I come instantly upon a thrilling paragraph entitled 'Tying a Hunting Stock'. Well, we can all dream, can't we, and there I am at once, in the mind's eye, all correctly kitted out for the shires and up on Moonbeam, with a 'Tally-ho' here and a 'Mornin', Lady Di' there and the centre of attraction as we, see how expert I am, draw the spinneys (one recalls those pre-war hunting reports in the *Times* and a memorable line which went 'Hounds found in Wriggly Bottom').

But despite this new fluency in the things that really matter, I cannot shut my eyes to the fact that one of my main difficulties is going to be how to get all the assorted technical lingo out with the correct air of authority and without, for such is my irreverent nature, a shy smile or two. There is also a grave risk of being seriously misunderstood and being considered to be dirty-minded. For example, in the Shooting section, the author paints a graphic verbal picture for the reader of a 'gun' (meaning one who fires a gun) in a covert shoot waiting tensely as the beaters' sticks come tapping their way through the trees towards him and 'tall' (by which we mean high, in the non-culinary sense) birds start coming over – pheasants, apparently, and of both sexes. What to do for the best (and here

*It's best to dress down in order 'to give an air of modesty'*

the sensitive must look away for a line or two)? 'You pull on a magnificent cock,' it says 'with your gun practically vertical.' This sort of phrase is, understandably, well beyond fastidious old me, and readers would certainly not wish me to risk myself further, but I have been able to work out that it means that you shoot at a male bird.

When not busily reminding me that trout fishing begins on March 1st, that The Oaks is run on the first Friday in June, that White's Club was established in 1693, that 1947 was a tip-top year for port, claret, burgundy and almost any other booze that you may care to name, my splendid book (*The Man's Book*, edited in 1958 by Colin Willock: keep your eyes peeled for it) is very informative about clothes and being, as some say, faultlessly groomed and 'whether or not to dress up or down to your personality'. Here's a teaser. If your personality is on the forceful side, it says that it's best to dress down in order 'to give an air of modesty'. Shy violets should, on the other hand, choose their fanciest suitings in order not to be ignored. As regards my own personality requirements, I shall just press quietly on with my grey off-the-peg uncrushable from the dear old Army and Navy Stores. At my time of life, whether this dresses me up or dresses me down is neither here nor there.

# Motley mishaps

There is one extremely important aspect of the last war that would appear to have been entirely overlooked and neglected by even the very best military historians. Thumb through the works of the greatly gifted Correlli Barnett, peruse the articles from the pen of the wholly admirable and delightful Michael Howard as one may, not a sign of the subject do we see and it is therefore left to me to raise the matter, an amateur historian if ever there was one and badly though what I have to say reflects on the government of the day. I am referring, of course, to the total absence, from 1940 onwards, of bananas.

By a process of reasoning that almost everybody can follow, no bananas means (and this would have been an ideal moment for employing the word 'ergo', if one were the kind of person who could at any point bear the word 'ergo') no banana skins. And no banana skins in our city roads and streets in the war years meant that there was nothing for old gentlemen to slip up on and measure their length and thus raise the spirits of any passing troops or civilians by giving them a hearty and valuable laugh. Laughs were then in very short supply and old gentlemen coming purlers would have pleased many and thereby shortened the war. How very short-sighted of the authorities not to have imported, instead of guns and ammunition and so on, crate after crate of the tasty fruit, with a request that, after use, the skins should be left lying out in the open. What a smack in the eye it would have been for old Hitler, eh what? What a morale-booster it could have furnished. I don't myself happen to find it amusing when poor old Mr Merryweather, hurrying to catch the 8.15, steps on a banana skin in Station Road and he and his bowler and gig-lamps and briefcase go flying in all directions, but then I have a strictly limited sense of humour which rigorously excludes any aspect, however piquant, of bananas.

I never, for example, know whether to laugh or cry in a theatre when things go badly wrong upon the stage. One is torn between hysteria and horror. Waste no sympathy, however, upon the players involved. Actors caught up in some grievous mishap are the first to start laughing and the last to stop and joyfully relate such misfortunes to each other down the years ('We were doing this Shaw thing at Nottingham and . . .'). I have been present on a number of occasions in theatres when not everything went according to Cocker (1631–75, reputed author of a popular arithmetic book and taken as a standard of orthodoxy). I must, I suppose, have been about twelve when a touring company of *Lilac Time* came to Colchester, where I was staying with my charming Essex grandmother. In those days, *Lilac Time* burgeoned each Christmas, just like *Peter Pan*, and was a reputably musical musical based on the life of Franz Schubert. Seats were booked (dress circle, natch) and off we went, rather grandly chauffeur-driven in a car called a Crossley which lived up to its name and was a sulky brute to start, crank as the chauffeur might. Anyway and in due course, down we sat and up went the curtain for Act I which revealed a riot of improbable-looking lilac in 'The Courtyard of a Lodging House' with the entire company singing like billy-o. Act II found us in 'A Sitting-room in Christian Veit's House', vases of lilac everywhere and heaps more singing. In the interval before Act III, the iron safety curtain was lowered to calm us all and in conformity with the legal requirements but when the moment came for it to be raised, it stuck when it had risen a mere four feet from the ground and nothing and nobody could persuade it to rise another inch. The theatre manager announced, to loud applause, that the company was nevertheless prepared to press on with Act III ('The Prater' and, I don't doubt, swags of lilac everywhere) and so the remainder of the tender love story unfolded itself to us in the form of headless bodies, moving now here, now there and belonging one never knew to quite whom, apart from that of the heroine, Lili, who, determined that we should not miss her top notes, bent down and shrieked them at us from underneath the curtain. My dear and roly-poly grandmother, a great giggler, was in fits throughout but I remember feeling, rather priggishly, I shouldn't wonder, more distressed than diverted.

But one occasion I did rather enjoy, so unusual was it and

*Lili determined that we should not miss her top notes . . .*

involving as it did no embarrassed human beings. It took place during a provincial and pre-London tour of an extremely elaborate musical play based on a famous novel, with a cast of eighty and numerous scenes and sets. Early on in the entertainment, various ominous back-stage bangings and lighting imperfections and hitches and unexplained pauses and loud whisperings betrayed the fact that all was not entirely well. At one point, after we had been sitting quietly in darkness for some time, bright lights suddenly came on to reveal an almost empty stage onto which there shyly entered from the right a piece of scenery. I should like to say that it glided on, but to tell the truth, judder on was what it did, propelled I suppose on some sort of trolley. It was quite a large piece of scenery and it showed us the side of a town house, with front door and window and steps and a small yew tree. It came to rest, in full view, and a respectful silence fell. We gazed politely at it, and it gazed right back at us. Was somebody going to come through the door or, even, clean the steps or prune the yew? Evidently not. The silence back stage was now complete and one felt that perhaps they had all gone out for a cup of tea or, perhaps, home. It is difficult to judge time accurately at such suspenseful moments but the piece of scenery (one cannot call anything so imposing 'a flat') must have been with us for a full two minutes, after which, obviously considering us a poor lot, it got on the move once more and creaked and juddered its way back into the wings, never to be seen again. The gallery, of course, cheered loudly. It was, heaven knows, their one chance.

There have been other memorable moments. I have been present when Edith Evans, half way through declaiming one of the late Queen Elizabeth's speeches, dried up completely and said, loudly and furiously and twice, '*What?*' to the indistinct prompter. Once in Lancashire, the male member of a pair of adagio dancers was so tipsy (we were enjoying an end-of-the-pier concert party) that his lady partner, held precariously aloft by him while she gracefully contorted, kept loudly and desperately hissing 'Put me down, you bloody fool!'. And I was once in Hamburg, at one of those operas that has a ballet inserted into it (can it have been *Faust?*), when one of the male dancers, gleefully hopping and kicking his legs up, sent one of his ballet shoes (those things that the more senior of us think of as 'pumps') flying vertically upwards until it was lost to view behind the proscenium arch. The *pensée* that 'what goes up must come down' was clearly visible on the faces of the other hoppers as they hopped on, and we all eagerly waited for the shoe to descend, but descend it never did. Got caught up somewhere, I suppose, though I dare say that our wartime bombs dislodged it satisfactorily. Older actors still speak of that remarkable moment when Mrs Patrick Campbell, touring in a play that required a snow scene (I think it may have been *Hannele*), purchased a newfangled German device that was said to provide the last word in artificial snow. She switched it on, all expectancy, on the first night and moved confidently stage centre, only to find herself being pelted with lumps of snow as large as cricket balls. She was to be seen, shrieking with laughter, fending off the missiles and shouting to the astonished audience 'And it cost me a *fortune!*'.

Sometimes a mishap occurs that requires the invention of extra dialogue to cover it, a particularly perilous undertaking when the play is very well known. In the early days of the open air theatre in Regent's Park, an actress friend of mine (let us call her Joyce) was appearing in a Shakespeare play. If the weather was inclement and the conditions windy, it was by no means easy for the performers to hear their cue and make their entrance, and one blustery evening Joyce was to be seen winding her way through shrubs and bushes and down a gravel path and then out onto the brightly lit raised lawn that served as a stage, only to find that she had arrived a whole scene too soon. Another actress already there, and legitimately, realised that Joyce must be got rid of as soon as possible and, summoning her most carrying tones, said loud and clear 'I have no business with thee. Go away!', a line that is not to be found in Shakespeare but which served to send Joyce hurrying back through the bushes, only to reappear once more shortly after when her actual cue came. 'Here she is again' said the audience to each other, much mystified by the elaborate comings and goings.

And sometimes, of course, disasters are purposely brought about. Some years ago, a now dead actress played Peter Pan and had contrived, foolishly as it turned out, to make herself very unpopular back stage (ceaseless pouts and complaints). Those responsible for flying her about decided to make life a little difficult for her and one evening in the Darlings' nursery, just when Peter was proudly demonstrating to Wendy his air-borne abilities and took off, making for the mantelpiece, he found that he had missed it by a foot or two and was scrabbling in a rather undignified manner up the wall.

# Behind the fringe

A theatre quiz for the somewhat older theatre buff and involving four ladies from the heyday of the post-Great War musical comedy stage and all of whose superb talents came into fragrant flower at more or less the same time. Let us call them A, B, C and D: and guess who. A had reddish hair, sang like a bird and could do marvellous imitations, including a particularly good one of D, who was at one time her sister-in-law. C's speciality was to sing slightly off key and she thereby managed to increase her charm, which was already phenomenal. B was by far the most beautiful and rather went in for 'waif' roles, a dazzling Cinderella permanently at the ball. They were all wonderful dancers and they could all, when necessary, kick. A could, I think, kick the highest (when in the centre of a chorus line, she could out-kick the lot and one looked – how very irritating for the rest of them – at nobody else). B, C and D went in for more graceful dancing (though A could get up on her toes), with B and D having a slight edge on C. Alas, only two of them, A and B, remain alive today and D, who in early days wore her hair in an attractive fringe and was able to achieve those difficult, circular high kicks, has only recently left us. The four are, of course, Binnie Hale, Dorothy Dickson, Gertrude Lawrence and Jessie Matthews, lovingly remembered as Binnie, Dotty, Gertie and Jessie.

Ah, but in what year in London could you have seen all four of them, with each in a success? Of course you've got it right – 1927 – with Miss Dickson in *Peggy-Ann* (boarding-house waif dreaming of a *de luxe* life on a yacht) at Daly's, Miss Lawrence as an immensely improbable American bootlegger in *Oh, Kay!*, a Gershwin musical at His Majesty's, Miss Hale touring the big suburban theatres in what was to become a smash-hit called *Mr Cinders* (Bobby Howes as a male waif), and Miss

Matthews in a brilliantly talented Cochran revue, *One Dam Thing After Another*, at the London Pavilion.

Much has been made in her obituaries of Miss Matthews's childhood in Soho, and rightly, for she looked in early days very much what she was, the bouncy product of a non-Mayfair London with an odd little wavery voice, an odd little face with large black-buttony eyes and which the dark fringe of hair suited to perfection. It was the sort of face that Chaplin used to make much of in his films, and at times she looked not unlike Jackie Coogan in *The Kid*, and he too had a raggle-taggle fringe peeping out from under that tattered cap. Though she had a perfect figure, it was somehow not a particularly feminine one. Elfin, that now rather despised word, is perhaps right for her. And when she moved, the effect was magical.

Here are two of many memorable theatrical moments before she too, like José Collins and Gertie Millar and Violet Loraine, passes into the mists. One of them was in that Cochran revue (the word 'Dam' was then only considered permissible when spelt like that and with the 'n' omitted: unbelievable, but true) when, after an entrancingly pretty American pianist called Edythe Baker had played, at a white grand piano, a Richard Rodgers show-stopper called 'My Heart Stood Still', Miss Matthews emerged from the wings and both sang and danced it, in a filmy, floating dress in which she seemed more airborne than earthbound. And then there was that item in the Coward and Cochran *This Year of Grace* in which she and Sonnie Hale sang 'A Room with a View', a moment that those who saw it are unlikely to forget. Of all the actresses in London, there seemed at the time to be nobody less suitable to take over, for BBC radio, the role of Mrs Dale, housewife super-ordinary of Parkwood Hill, but she brought it triumphantly off. A very unusual performer.

If, in 1927, you had already seen all those four charmers, there were plenty of other treats available. At the Playhouse, when the house lights first lowered and then went out, one was startled to hear, in the darkness, the sound of a revolver firing and when the curtain dramatically rose, there was the beautiful Gladys Cooper, looking distraught on the verandah of a Malayan bungalow and emptying, as they used to say, a wicked-looking little Colt (ditto) into an admirable and inoffensive actor called S. J. Warmington. With splendid aim and drawing a fine bead, Miss Cooper got him with the very first shot, a faultless bull's-eye that would have drawn admiring gasps at Bisley. But why then, as his lifeless body slumped with a thump to the floor, did she continue to pump (and they used to say that too) bullet after bullet into the corpse? Ah, why indeed? Mr Warmington, she told the local police, had, while her husband was away in Singapore, attempted amorous familiarities, but of course those of us who had read Somerset Maugham's *The Letter* knew better. Mr W was her former lover who had thrown her over for a native woman and the bullets were intended as a tactful little reminder and corrective.

There were, whichever way you looked, stars to be seen – real, proper, seasoned stars (when I hear a 20-year-old, who can neither sing nor twang but who jumps about a bit in a T-shirt and what look like rather grubby gym shoes, described by a confrère as 'one of the All Time Greats' I feel what the Americans call 'sick to my stomach': forgive it, and put it down to my age, or something). There was Leslie Henson pulling those lovely, cod-like faces in *Lady Luck*. There was Edith Day, a willing bundle ('Methinks the lady doth protest too little'), being carried off in the strong arms of the Red Shadow in *The Desert Song* at what was always called The Lane. There was a Lonsdale comedy and Sidney Howard's excellent *The Silver Cord*. There was *The Vagabond King* at the Winter Garden, and Ben Travers at the Aldwych and, for some of us, all was well with our theatre world.

# Coming clean

One of the many hidden advantages of 'getting on' is that sufferers from either seasickness or shyness or both will find their afflictions decreasing in potency. When, fairly recently, I found myself happily tucking into roast pork and buttery carrots in the middle of an extremely disturbed Bay of Biscay (such a test for the strongest stomach), I merely blessed my advancing years and called for a further dollop of crackling. Though in my youth and since, Bovril splendidly prevented that purely physical sinking feeling, it could do nothing for one's nerves on social occasions and, when entering a room largely full of strangers, finding a hostess advancing on one with 'Now, whom don't you know?' But nowadays I wouldn't give a hoot.

Despite a robust appearance, a passion for amateur theatricals and, usually, an inanely smiling face, I was when young quite excessively shy. Going, as one frequently did in the hols, to stay with the parents of kind school-friends, I was continually a prey to nervous agitations. Though always temporarily reassured on arrival by a charming mother and a hearty tea (no tea was then a tea that did not provide ginger snaps and a dish of cape gooseberry jam), there were several further worries to plague one. In pre-war houses of the older sort, lavatories were few and far between and were customarily limited to a single mahogany throne next to the single bathroom. When, I used to wonder, would be the absolutely ideal moment for visiting it? Should one loudly cough on approaching it so that any possible occupant could cough right back at one and thus avoid noisy bolted-door rattlings? What if I required to go during the night? Would my schoolfriend's father, on his return from work, turn out to be grumpy or genial? Geniality was not the first thing that I associated with my own father on his return from a gruelling day in the City.

*When, I used to wonder, would be the absolutely ideal
moment for visiting it?*

There was one hazard with which I never learned to cope. In
the social circles in which we moved, there was, while staying
away, only one method of being awoken to face a new day. On
the very tick of 8 a.m. a trimly uniformed housemaid appeared
in one's bedroom, rattled back the curtains and departed,
leaving at the bedside a cup of tea and a very large and thin slice
of bread-and-butter. In those days, to eat or drink the very
moment I woke up made me feel sick. There was therefore no
question of either sipping or munching. How, then, to dispose
of this nutritional windfall? It never for one moment occurred
to me to beg my hostess not to bother with such comforts. I
was anyhow far too shy to do so and I somehow felt that it
would be both rude and ungrateful. To fold the bread-and-
butter and conceal it within a dirty handkerchief in my suitcase
was easy enough, but how to get rid of the tea? I could hardly
be found carrying it, loudly coughing, to the lavatory, and to
tip it into the chamber-pot beneath the bed might have caused
the household to suspect a severe intestinal malfunction re-

quiring instant hospitalization. So I used to creep to the window and empty the cup onto the lawn or flower-bed beneath. Once, while doing this, a window suddenly shot open on the ground floor and the tea descended in a steaming brown cascade onto the head of the very housemaid who had brought it up. One of the risks of her profession, of course, but guilt forced me to double her tip (five shillings) and avoid her wounded gaze for the rest of my visit.

Shyness inhibited speech, and fear did much the same. Are present-day children ever shy and frightened as we often were? I very much doubt it, and a good thing too. At my prep school on the Hampshire coast, a great business was made of 'owning up' to various crimes. Only a lunatic would have owned up ahead of time, so to speak, as the misdemeanour might still go unnoticed. Hardly a week passed without the entire school being assembled in the dining-hall and somebody being asked to own up to a broken window, a cracked tooth-mug or a plate of pat-a-cakes mysteriously missing from Matron's snuggery. The headmaster in a rage was an alarming spectacle and fright, as often as not, produced in the potential criminals nothing but an uneasy silence.

We did have, however, a great boon in the shape of a matchless school-fellow called Williamson. He was, whether guilty or not, a dedicated owner-up. He felt it to be no more than his duty for, to combat the rigours of our scholastic surroundings (pretty ghastly) and the really rather depressing routines (completely deadly), he had invented for himself a dream world in which he was of royal blood, and the best blood at that. For a whole term he managed to persuade himself that he was actually the King and that George V was nothing but a very shady impostor. This, naturally, gave him a serene look. He was obviously far above such pettinesses as cracked pottery. So he took, as another, our sins upon himself. He used, for his dining-hall confessions, to take a pace forward and the royal way in which his 'It was I, headmaster' rang out was much admired. He used sportingly to take in his stride the beating which often followed (two extra strokes for the impertinence of saying 'Headmaster' instead of 'sir'). What scorn he would have had for all the modern twaddle about the 'indignity', or whatever, of this handy method of punishment. And then, with his cares of state temporarily shelved and moving freely amongst us in informal and unbuttoned mood, he could sometimes be persuaded to give us his piercing treble rendering of 'Love Will Find A Way' from the *Maid of the Mountains*, a noise which used comfortably to reach the distant staff quarters and bring the staff hurrying to protest.

What asses those who direct our lives are never, and with no risk of six of the best, to own up to their own inadequacies, mistakes and shortcomings. There is nothing so disarming as a frank confession of total failure. I would like all persons wishful to push themselves forward into public life first to be forced to sit a 'Knowledge of Human Nature' exam, those with less than 90% to be instantly expelled. So few leading politicians appear to have the very slightest idea what the average human being is *like*. The prime minister has only to come on the box and, looking apologetic for once, detail the past year's main disasters (there is, God knows, a choice) to win all hearts. 'He's human, after all' would echo from lip to lip.

But nobody will ever own up and meanwhile things go from bad to worse, which brings me by a natural transition to the Post Office. Gone for ever is the Sunday Post. Clear to all is the fact that this once great institution is now run solely for the benefit of those who man it. And now there is a fresh cause for concern. I have in the last few months been carrying out a private investigation into what happens to 9p letters posted on a Friday and either to or from London. You will find, if you do the same, that nothing very much happens to them. A large majority, in my sad experience, now stays right where it is.

I am thinking of supplying free to the Post Office for erection in all sorting offices, a large coloured poster featuring a dear old granny and a sweet little kiddy both blubbing their eyes out. Mum, away from home, you see, and visiting a sick sister has written but nothing has arrived (through the window, Postman Joe can be seen passing the gate). Beneath this touching picture are the words REMEMBER, IF YOU DELAY A LETTER YOU MAY BREAK A HEART. Who could resist such a moving reminder? It would be bound to result in a furious flurry of activity, even on a Friday.

# Pass the spuds

Under a headline which read, and how accurately, POPULAR POTATO, the *Daily Telegraph*, ever first in the field with All The News That Matters, announced to its startled readers on February 27th that 'the average Briton ate 2108 lb of potatoes last year, seven pounds more than in 1978.' This works out at somewhere between what we call a short ton (2000 lb) and a long ton (2240) and kindly don't expect me to have any truck with that awful foreign word 'tonne', which sounds like somebody pronouncing 'one' as 'wan' (it will be, as far as I am concerned, tons and yards and pints and miles till the day I die). Although know-alls will, when they see that figure of 2108 (mathematics has always been a bit of a bother but this seems to come to nearly six pounds of potatoes per head per day), hasten to claim that this is a misprint for a mere 210 lbs a year, a piffling intake of healthful starch, I prefer to regard 2108 lbs as being the correct figure, blindly devoted as I am to the deliciously nutritious tuber.

Although my mother knew what was what in the way of good straight English food and ordered and supervised it to perfection, at home and in my youth we were never very adventuresome with potatoes. They arrived boiled. They arrived mashed. On Sunday evenings they arrived in their jackets. New potatoes made their bow gleaming with butter and lavishly parsley-sprinkled, and a joint of roast beef reached the table with, naturally, roast potatoes clustering round its base, like youthful servers round a lordly and well-liking Bishop. Sauté potatoes appeared on rare occasions (that foreign adjective was suspicious) but that was about it. Any attempt on the part of the cook to branch out and dish up something relatively simple such as potatoes *Lyonnaises* (roughly the same as sauté only with the tasty addition of chopped onions) would not have pleased my father. 'What are these, may I ask?' On being told that they were called *Lyonnaises* and were therefore a French invention, he would have refused them. One knew all about France, thank you very much, a country where nobody washed, where the tin, kerbside gentlemen's retiring-places concealed all too little and permitted conversation ('*Ça va, Hercule?*') with passers-by when the occupant should have been solely concerned with the matter in hand, a country where they lived on frogs and gazed lasciviously at saucy picture post-cards.

But it was of course in France that one first discovered the endless varieties of culinary treatment (there are said to be over 200) that can be applied to the humble potato or, as we are now across the Channel, *la pomme de terre humble*. Before going up to Cambridge in 1928, my father kindly swallowed his dislike and distrust of the French and sent me off, in the interests of education, to spend the summer with a French family on the outskirts of Grenoble. The family consisted of three spinster sisters ('of a certain age', as they tactfully put it) and the food was admirable. Potatoes appeared in all sorts of delicious disguises and to enjoy them there were, with me, five or six resident students hungrily gathered together.

They reached the table in a fireproof dish (and it is to the potatoes that I am referring), layered with Gruyère, flavoured with garlic, moistened with chicken stock and delightfully browned in the oven. They arrived miraculously blended with bacon and leeks and nestling in a cheese sauce. They entered in a savoury mixture of cream cheese, hard-boiled eggs and chives, with parsley sprigs here and there. They came masked with a white sauce tasting of lemon and calling themselves *à la Maître d'Hôtel*. When they appeared in their jackets, you could bet your bottom *franc* that they were not alone and that within their mashed and buttered interiors one would find lurking such excitements as flaked fish or chopped anchovies or diced cooked meat or, surprisingly good, kidneys. Meanwhile, and while munching, one strove to remember why one was there and to enliven the occasion with interesting snippets of chat – '*Dans les pièces de Molière, moi je trouve que . . .*' or, when running short of stimulating *pensées*, '*Quel beau jour!*'

And then one sensational day, drama struck (nothing to do with the potatoes, though a single potato did have its part to play). Although we English students had signed on, so to speak, for four months, the European ones supplied by a

*Where the tin kerbside gentlemen's retiring place is*

foreign branch of the University and mainly Swedish, with a sprinkling of Danes, tended to come and go for shorter periods and one day we found seated at the lunch table a girl of, I suppose, twenty with dazzling fair hair and a worldly look to her – a girl, and yet not a girl, if you follow me. We also found frost in the normally cheerful atmosphere. Of the three sisters, one of them, Mlle Alice, was bedridden and permanently absent, but the other two, Mlles Cécile and Berthe, were present and looking daggers. In an icy chill, formal introductions were made – '*Permettez-moi de vous présenter Fräulein Hulda Bendix de Berlin.*' German! By some fearful mischance, a Hun was in our midst, for who, remembering Attila, could think of them otherwise? The war had been over a mere ten years, the sisters had lost a brother, Pierre, and numerous other relations in it and were certainly not going to forget the fact. The meal began in a dreadful silence. Potatoes (I do not now recall how cooked) came and went. Conversation was stilted (I gave, I expect and as was my jolly way, my customary weather report). Hulda finished her glass of wine and, an unheard-of act of effrontery, asked, like Oliver, for more. It was reluctantly supplied, and with a look that would have done credit to the Borgias.

The minute any meal was over, Hulda made for the tram that ran along the bottom of our road and set off for the centre of Grenoble. Why? Ah, why indeed! Meanwhile the implacable sisters continued with their persecutions. They pretended not to hear when Hulda, struggling to learn polite French conversation, spoke. They gave her short commons. They watered, I suspect, her wine. They missed no chance of speaking insultingly of the Fatherland, and a photograph of poor, uniformed Pierre, *mort pour la patrie*, was prominently placed so that it could glare at Hulda. Then news came, I know not whence but perhaps a Swede out shopping spotted her, that Hulda's twice-daily destination was a large and *de luxe* Grenoble hotel. Again, why?

I did not, alas, witness the final dénouement, having decided on that particular evening to go to a performance by a touring company of *No No Nanette*, fully recognisable in French as *Non Non Nanette*, but next day my fellow students hastened to supply me with the breathtaking details. Poor Hulda, her spirit finally broken, had been seen to be tearful for most of the day and at the evening meal was just picking at her food when suddenly the front door was heard to open, heavy footsteps crossed the hall and a very large and angry middle-aged German gentleman burst into the room and let fly, in the language of Goethe but not in his words, a torrent of abuse directed, as they cowered back, at our two hostesses. Hulda's father come to complain, you suppose? Not a bit of it. Hulda's sugar-daddy it was who, anxious to install his mistress in both a Berlin flat and polite society, had decided to provide her with a smattering of French and, what is more, to stay nearby in order to supervise the undertaking and comfort Hulda from time to time, and vice versa. When the shameful situation had become crystal clear to all, Mlle Cécile let out a scream, while Mlle Berthe clutched, a favourite gesture, her heart. And Hulda, in floods of defiant tears, resourcefully picked up a jacket potato and threw it at Berthe (the larger of the two and therefore the better target) but, even with the fine traditions of Krupps armaments behind her, she missed and her missile burst on poor old Pierre, the final insult. You would probably like to know whether the jacket potato contained fish or egg or meat or anchovies but this valuable detail is, I fear, not now available.

# Play the game

How very true it is that every day of your life you can, if blessed with an alert mind, a sharp intelligence and questing mental antennae, gifts that Blind Fortune has seen fit to bestow (yes, Ben Jonson) on a privileged few of us, learn something of interest and can pop away yet another factual nugget in Memory's Treasure-Chest to cherish on long winter evenings, and it was only yesterday that I discovered that, in 1831, W. G. Grace's mother, seated in a chair, made a daring flight by giant box-kite across the Avon Gorge. Meanwhile her schoolmaster uncle, Alfred Pocock, was busy inventing a caning machine which, presumably steam-driven, administered the required number of thwacks and was impervious to screams, a real boon to the more sensitive members of the teaching profession. Perhaps those supporters of capital punishment who are worried about the human element involved could produce a sort of Heath Robinson contraption on similar Pocock lines ('Insert subject at doorway marked A, feed in hempen rope at aperture B, press button C and stand well back').

For the benefit of those few readers who may never have heard of either W. G. Grace or his spirited airborne and chairborne mama, let me explain that he was the Victorian father of Cricket As We Know It Today, a dashing performer both at the crease and while thundering up to deliver the leather (it's called bowling), a six foot bearded giant and a world-wide celebrity. As late as 1924 (he died in 1915, partly from a Zeppelin-induced stroke) when I went as a boy to Oundle School, his name was still spoken of in awed tones for we had had his son, W. G. Junior, on the staff, and our splendid school chaplain, The Rev M. W. Brown, had once played wicket-keeper to the great W. G. himself and could quite easily be coaxed during lessons to tell us yet again the

*made a daring flight by giant box kite across the Avon Gorge*

highlights of this rewarding experience rather than dispense the mathematics for which we were gathered together. The late Maurice Richardson, a contemporary of mine at Oundle, always maintained that one of Mr Brown's sermons contained the words, 'Jesus was a gentleman. He played with a straight bat and stood up to the bowling.' And what's wrong with that, may I ask? There were, after all, eleven reliable disciples and a very fine team they might have made (I seem to see James, son of Zebedee, as longstop and Simon the Canaanite going in at No 5).

By now two questions will be uppermost in readers' minds and the first of course is, to what extent did the Grace ambience at Oundle rub off on me as a youthful cricketer and the immediate answer is, I fear, 'not very noticeably', though at one point I did achieve an elevation from the very lowest butterfinger ranks. Boys not chosen to play either for school teams (oh the glory of going out to bat on our beautiful ground, The Square, and facing the MCC or some such!) or for their two house teams were relegated to what was called The Remainder Game, situated on sloping ground near The Armoury, a building of minimal architectural appeal and which housed rifles. Here, unsupervised and with every show of reluctance, forty or so flannelled fumblers picked up sides and managed as worst they could. It made a dispiriting and profitless afternoon and it was with some relief that I found myself promoted to my house's second XI (is my 3 Not Out against School House still remembered? I dare say they speak of it yet).

And doubtless the second question is, whence comes my almost encyclopaedic knowledge of Dr W. G. Grace, a medical man of whom, so seldom can he have been available during the months of King Willow's reign, one would have been rather relieved not to be a patient. My knowledge comes from the admirable pen and fine talents for research of Eric Midwinter, an unsuitable surname to conjure with in cricketing circles but his famous forebear, W. E. Midwinter, was the only player ever to represent, in Test Matches, both Australia and England, and here, in *W. G. Grace, His Life and Times* (Allen & Unwin, £9.95), Mr Midwinter tells all, and much of it will come as a deep shock to those who, starry-eyed, have placed the doctor on a pedestal for there seems little doubt that both on the field and off he was really quite fairly horrid, besides being a good bit lacking in what the advertisements call 'personal freshness'.

'Pavilion, you!', he would yell, a finger dramatically pointing, to a batsman who, considering his dismissal unfair, was reluctant to leave the centre of things. And when in the Oval pavilion himself and one of his team was given 'out', he screamed from the balcony, like an odious child in a tantrum, 'Shan't have it, can't have it, and won't have it'. And of his own reluctance to remove himself, the *Sportsman* of 1912 commented acidly on 'the weakness of W. G. for dwelling at the wicket after the umpire's decision.' Unwashed and grubby, it was the opinion of the Viscount Cobham of the day that Grace's was 'one of the dirtiest necks I have ever kept wicket behind.' Managing miraculously to hover, in a manner that even Pocock might have envied, for it was he of the box-kite, somewhere midway between the ranks of amateur and professional players, he amassed from cricket and between the years 1870 and 1910, not less than £120,000, equal today to millions.

And yet and yet, the cricketing achievements are stupefying. Turning the scales at 15 stone and 'full of life and vim' as the press of the day had it, in the five seasons of 1868 to 1872 he scored 21,628 runs at an average of 55, and mostly on wickets that were very far from perfect. In the eight days of one county match, he scored 839 runs for an average of 419.5, and he was as deadly with the ball as with the bat. Happy snaps of various whiskery players and teams decorate Mr Midwinter's excellent text, making the book a must for all serious-minded followers of the game and who can face the fact that an idol had feet of clay, even though the feet were encased in size 14 cricketing boots.

# Four cheers

I have always, as regular readers will know, ranged pretty widely subjectwise in this column, and those who don't much care for words with -wise tacked onto them must realise that I am only trying to give a bit of a modern fillip to a style that may possibly have seemed sometimes a trifle old-fashioned and in need of being, like those potatoes in bags, crisped. Anyway, the variety of topics that have here been, from time to time, under discussion amazes even me – Mrs Thatcher's diet, the works of Angela Brazil, A New Way With Carrots, the Indian mutiny, Richard II, Vim and Harpic, Hamlet, Typhoo tea, poor old Onan and so on, the keen and well-stocked mind darting now here, now there. Hitherto, however, I have not much dealt with international matters of importance, preferring to leave them to wiser (if that's what I mean) heads that mine, and if I now make mention of Gibraltar it is partly to use it as a springboard for a later discussion of a more joyous affair altogether and partly because I fancy that I have stumbled on the real cause of the King of Spain's displeasure and refusal to turn up, smiling and clutching a gift-wrapped gift, at the royal wedding on 29 July.

Mind you, and fair is fair, I do see how quite tremendously irritating it must be to have fortified foreigners perched on a largish rock a mere stone's throw from one's shores. Picture if you will a Spanish colony holding on firmly to Cowes, brightest jewel in the crown of the Isle of Wight (with Ventnor a close second), their guns all trained and prepared to pepper Portsmouth, and with a Customs barrier ('Kindly have all passports ready') in the High Street and just this side of the Co-op, if such there be. I rather think, however, that our continued presence in their portion of the Mediterranean is not what occasioned the royal huffiness and that the clue lies in a sentence thrown off on 29 July by a BBC announcer (can it have been Tom Fleming, the excellent provider of such a flowing feast of information and piquant fact?). 'It was to St Paul's,' the voice said, 'that Queen Elizabeth the First came to offer up her humble thanks for the defeat of the Spanish Armada in 1588.' There you are, you see! Now we know the real reason why he wouldn't come. Not Gibraltar at all but something far less reputable and which can be summed up in just the one word. Sulks.

And now to the marvellously cheering event on Wednesday 29 July and which the King was such an old silly-billy to miss. Fellow reporters in this neck of the NS woods, busy with what are perhaps weightier matters and therefore and understandably rather less inclined than I to rejoice about anything at all, have not found time or space to express what so very many feel (though some would rather die than admit it) and therefore it is left to me to say how heartening, warm, uplifting, enjoyable, moving, life-enchancing, proud-making and totally splendiferous the entire day and happy happening were.

Here at 'Myrtlebank', where I was glad to be joined by friends, we were all astir with the dawn and by the time the first telly flickerings started to come through we were in our viewing positions and grouped expectantly round the Baird 15-incher (colour, natch), hot coffee, beef sandwiches and hankies at the ready – quite impossible not to blub from time to time and, where I was sitting, lumps in the throat were two a penny. Apart from an occasional dash to the bathroom where Optrex, such a soothing and anticongestive boon in cases of eye-soreness, was freely available to one and all, we sat it out, entranced and bewitched, to the end. Then a nourishing dinner – mulligatawny soup, roast shoulder and the last of the rasps – followed by an early and contented bed with the sandman paying his grainy call on the tick of 10 p.m.

On a famous occasion, the first night of *Cavalcade*, Mr Coward, summoned before the curtain, had this to say: 'I hope that this play has made you feel that, in spite of the troublous times we are living in, it is still pretty exciting to be English.' That was 1931, not 1981. Six years later, at the Coronation of George VI, an American lady, rising from her stand seat when all was over, was heard to say, as she wiped her streaming eyes, 'God knows why we ever cut loose.' The cynical and dull of soul will find substance here for sneers but I suspect that these sad scoffers are far fewer than might be imagined.

It cannot be easy to combine unassailable dignity with an out-giving friendliness but the principal players always achieve it to perfection. The extraordinary efficiency of the stage-managing was to be marvelled at, the only anxious moment being the plucky but tottery Earl's progress up the aisle (and I bet that there were contingency plans, code-name OOOPS!, in case of a tumble). Even anti-monarchists must have enjoyed the superb fireworks that kicked the whole thing so dazzlingly off, and do even their hard hearts not beat a little faster at the mere idea of a line of beacon fires blazing from summit to summit?

One had random thoughts. Was the bride's 25-foot train, so skilfully managed by Lady Sarah Armstrong-Jones, perhaps just eight feet too long? Princess Anne, so suited by Mother-hood, stirred a music-hall memory ('Where did you get that hat, where did you get that tile?'). Was that the first royal kiss ever exhibited to the public on the balcony? What had the horses had for breakfast, and when? Would the fact that the bride got the bridegroom's Christian names in the wrong order mean that the whole ceremony was null and void and illegal and would have to be done all over again at another time (hoo-ray!)?

Search as one might in the crowd, there was not a face that was not smiling, and the average age seemed to be, surprising-ly, in the mid-twenties. Surely something that gives such pure pleasure to so many cannot be wholly, or even partly, wrong.